# RIVERS
## OF MY
# LIFE

John Burns

ISBN 979-8-89485-021-4 (Paperback)
ISBN 979-8-89485-022-1 (Digital)

Covenant Books
11661 Hwy 707
Murrells Inlet, SC 29576
www.covenantbooks.com

*To the men of Task Force Ranger and Bravo
Company 3/75 Ranger Regiment.
To Jesus Christ for saving me from myself.*

# PREFACE

Why rivers? As I began to contemplate the command of Paul to redeem the time in our lives, I fully began to look at the places where life became real to me. Littered in my past were great rivers. I began to look for the God of creation, beside the waters of the rivers of my entire life.

Nothing tells the story of time like the gift of a river. Whether meandering through a valley or raging through a town established upon its banks, rivers lead to history revealed. The rivers of my life reveal just what was going on in my life: on the surface and in the spirit and soul God desired to inhabit.

It is the rivers of my life that caused me to question every pre-supposition and social norm governing our civilization. Rivers are the foundation upon which the classroom of my life unfolded, with God our creator as my greatest teacher.

Rivers point to the foundation of civilization in human history. To unlock the pivotal part that rivers play in all our lives is to begin to understand the sovereignty of God the creator.

I believe rivers point to intelligent design. Understanding the source of the rivers in our own life leads to a lifetime of fellowship to the creator who gave us these amazing centers of power.

To harness a river has always been the goal of humanity. To unleash rivers of living water has always been the goal of God for his creation. The foundation for the entire creation is living water, both physically and spiritually. Christ crucified is the source of both.

To master the rivers of my life and compare them to the great rivers found in the Bible is to unlock secrets from God as he reveals his single intention for the world he alone created. Rivers are both a source of cursing and a source of blessing, both controlled by the God of creation.

The source of the rivers in my life revealed that storms are what form great rivers. The source of the living water revealed begins with a storm. The storm releases great torrents of water in the form of rain and snow. It is in the storms of life that we first learn to call out to God our creator.

The goal is the mountaintop of life. Literal mountains contain the secret to understanding the human condition. No one cries out to God while on top of the mountain. It is in the valleys of life that we learn to ask God for the waters of refreshing, found beside the still waters, where the Messiah leads those he loves.

Rivers of water bring life. The river meanders from its source in the mountaintop, then provides refreshment along the way as it empties into one of the great seas created by God for our provision.

I took the great rivers in my life for granted as I meandered through life wondering if God existed. The rivers began to reveal that God always existed in my life. I needed the humility to glean his perfect will for my life by rediscovering the rivers that played the primary role in getting me to where I am today.

My story begins outside Philadelphia, Pennsylvania, along the Delaware River, and the place of my nativity. Along the way, we will travel to twenty-two rivers in forty-two countries on five continents. Our destination is the Jordan River in Israel.

This is a story of refreshment. My life is the subject, creation is the classroom, and Elohim is the creator and my greatest teacher. The owners' manual and warranty deed for my life is the Bible. The Bible alone points to every river in my life.

The most preposterous debt payment plan in human history has been revealed to me along the banks of the world's great rivers and a few smaller rivers God had mercy to allow me to experience. The lessons learned all point to the mercy and grace provided by God on the cross at Calvary.

The Bible is a book which speaks of rivers of living water. The metaphorical view leads to overspiritualization of the messes we find ourselves in throughout life. Those choices reveal if Jesus Christ is the foundation for every riverbed upon which the waters of refreshing flow, polishing lively stones, which themselves unlock history and time. The greatest revelation I have received from the Bible is called expositional constancy.

Stones, rivers, worms, scarlet threads, Gentile brides, the mark of Cain, and the tabernacle in scripture reveal through clear patterns how an intelligent designer called God wrote the whole book!

The sevenfold fingerprint on the entire book we believers call the Bible should convince the greatest skeptic if their goal is to confront their own presuppositions with the end game of learning.

Ignorance is to condemn without investigating. I, too, was an incredible agnostic. Thankfully I never stopped questioning the existence of a creator, with complete sovereignty over every aspect of creation, both good and bad, and how they exist solely for the purpose of discovering the loving God, who went out of his way to redeem creation from the hands of a usurper, a fallen angel.

The rivers of my life are where I discovered our creator and where the greatest life lessons became reality. I have experienced peace and warfare along great rivers. They are this world's greatest teacher.

Nothing in nature reveals the mind of the intelligent designer of our world like the rivers we have built our world upon. The only one that is missing is the only one that matters.

All we must do is acknowledge just how far each one of us has gone to worship this creation, more than worship God the creator. The waters of refreshing will flow forth from the mountain of God when we acknowledge God in the valleys and on the mountaintops of this life!

*He was crucified upon a cross of wood, yet he created the hill upon which it stood. He is alive forevermore, and he is returning for his virgin bride very soon.*

Rangers Lead the Way! (RLTW)
October 8, 2022

# MERCY

# THE DELAWARE RIVER

The place of my nativity is called Darby township, in Delaware county, Pennsylvania. My neighborhood is called Briarcliffe, a predominantly Roman Catholic diocese with a public school system sharing our space. Religion was shared between Catholics, Protestants, and Jews. It seems on the surface like utopia on earth. Undergirding it all were labor unions, tradesmen, accountants, car salesmen, junkies, veterans, and cops. Most were also volunteer firemen in the neighborhood as well.

Inherent prejudice abounded in the neighborhood I would grow up in. My Catholic school and church were all White Catholics. The public school was predominantly White until desegregation reached our county in 1983.

They merged schools that had been segregated. While looking good on the surface, all humans possess fears about people who do not look like them. America must confront the eugenic makeup of our society, and education system, if we are ever going to return to pragmatism and better race relations.

Having high school children who have never spent time with children who do not look like them to automatically accept each other turned out to be the place our global-minded government targeted to instill the vision of a global utopia as they set about destroying our moral fabric.

It was through failure in Catholic high school that my mind turned to the future as I enrolled in public education. I had witnessed so much hypocrisy being practiced by people claiming a monopoly on the idea of God that I bowed out of church and the religion of my ancestors.

I decided to worship the religion of this world. Capitalism and the promise of upward mobility became the source of my newfound religion. I enrolled in vo-tech and began to work with my grandfather by the age of thirteen.

The trades he taught me would enable me to begin making real money while still in high school. I began to think quitting school was my best option while making great money weekly. My grandfather and father talked me into joining the Army Reserves to get some structure in my life.

By eleventh grade, I was making four hundred dollars a week in 1983. Narcotics and alcohol were both easily purchased. I had become enthralled with the night life. Cocaine, angel dust, and eventually heroin entered my life and would haunt me for the next thirty-plus years.

The Army Reserve contract saved my life and changed my future trajectory. I would attend basic training in June of 1985 and return home to participate in reserve drills until returning to Advanced Infantry Training (AIT) in June 1986. A temporary reprieve from drugs and alcohol would see me experience limited success in the reserves.

After returning from AIT in the summer of 1986, I reenrolled in Catholic school, more so to please my parents than succeed. I had set my sights on returning to public school and the chance to continue partying until I could take the GED test and enlist full-time in the Army.

I quit school and returned to work doing masonry construction full-time. Many people looked out for me and helped keep me out of most trouble. I returned to using narcotics and would end up as a heroin addict for a time before enlisting to leave in 1987.

January of 1987 would see nineteen-year-old addict John Burns learn a skill he wishes he never learned. I needed more money than I was making to feed my heroin addiction, so I turned to an older friend who would teach me to steal cars from the airport.

We became efficient at targeting the odd couple who would walk each other into the airport as their car was left running, or not. We could steal a car in about eleven seconds. Depending on the make and model, above six hundred dollars was paid by any number of body shops or junkyards to feed our habits.

Along the way, I somehow began to question the narrative about my biological mother's fall from grace and divorce from my father. I was told of her addiction and abandonment of her kids while my father answered his draft notice. What I questioned was, Why?

I was told my mother was Roman Catholic. I questioned that once I visited my biological grandparents' home in New Jersey at the behest of my dad's mom. Only a grandmother understands how much children need both parents in their lives and their parents' parents!

My grandparents ended up being Ukrainian immigrants who came here with their parents fleeing Russian persecution beginning sometime in the early 1900s. They were Jewish, not Roman Catholic. They did what most Jews did while escaping: hide their identity and adopt Roman Catholic names!

Their past is their religion, and their past is the plight of the people who can claim actual family ties to the Messiah that many people of faith believe in. My ancestors on my mother's side alone held the key to God's pleasing, perfect will for my life.

My love for scripture began as a young man growing up on a creek that flowed into the mighty Delaware River in Philadelphia. This city is the true source of my Christian patriotism. The Bible I began reading was the Bible George Washington placed his hand on when he pledged allegiance as our nation's first president.

This Bible was meant to be absorbed over the course of a lifetime. It happens to be the only book that was conceived entirely outside of how we humans experience time. Its precepts were given by the creator of the universe, and his promises are all eternal.

The most preposterous debt payment plan in human history began to be revealed to me early in my life and while in the valleys, not on top of any mountain. I am thankful I never gave up on God then, and I am thankful I was able to find out if what the Bible says is more important than any tradition we cling to.

The seeds of mercy over my life were first watered by the God, who intended one day to save me from my own terrible thinking. My life is a testimony to whom much is given, much is to be expected. God saved me from myself, and it began along the Delaware River.

I am indebted to my parents for allowing me to experience the majesty of refreshment provided by rivers!

October 8, 2022

\*\*\*\*\*

After meeting my biological grandparents at the age of five, seeds were planted that would not bear fruit in my life until I left behind totally the land of my nativity.

The lessons learned in Briarcliffe would carry me well into my forties before I had put to bed addiction, religion, capitalism, ancestor worship, and government as God. My life now revolves around every word of scripture.

I was a completely confused child. Although my father would work tirelessly to support his family monetarily, turning his children over to an education system where God is not the centerpiece had lasting implications long into his children's lives.

Growing up without my biological mother turned out to be a blessing. I would learn late in life that I shared her taste for narcotics and her desire for rebellion. My relationship to women was one of sexuality at a young age and selfishness in relationship to myself.

Very early on in Catholic school, I bought into the outward piety model for Catholic conduct. Problem was, the Bible says Jesus Christ died for sinners, of which I felt I was one. The Bible talked of one mediator between God and man, the Lord Jesus Christ. No need for a priest.

Everything in Catholicism revolved around what I did, not what God was doing. Legalism had replaced relationship to the Messiah. Angels are worshipped, and Roman holidays replaced the holidays Jesus Christ celebrated during his lifetime.

I began to realize early on why God told Abram of Chaldea to leave the land of his nativity and leave the gods of his parents in Babylon. I began to feel as though something was missing in my life, and the Catholic religion and catechism made me feel unworthy of salvation.

I was drilled in the Ten Commandments and taught about Mary, the virgin mother of Jesus, whom the Catholic church has wrongly placed above Jesus and God. The deification of the woman goes back to Nimrod and Semiramis in Babylon, where the Catholic church has its true foundations.

It made no sense to me that the Bible talked of one man with one woman for life producing godly seed. The Bible does not mention men becoming voluntarily celibate and women becoming voluntary virgins. This denies God access to the womb of women, and it makes men incredibly irresponsible and selfish.

God's perfect will is for all men to come to the knowledge of Jesus Christ. His pattern is to have human reproduction provide God with worshippers. Pagan priests from Babylon planted the seeds that have perverted the perfect will of God for humanity.

I was taught that covetousness was ungodly, yet we teach our children to beg on their birthdays and every other Roman holiday that has migrated from Babylon.

We parade our daughters in beauty pageants while never acknowledging their inner qualities. The mercy and grace of God in women has been replaced with the desire to replace men as the breadwinners and protectors of the family unit.

My childhood dreams were interrupted when my father and mother divorced. Pundits may say that I was too young to remember, while God alone says "Train up a child in the way they should go and when they are old, they will not depart from it" (Proverbs 22:6 KJV).

The Bible reveals the heart and mind of God when it comes to children. Isaiah teaches us that God reveals his word to all those taken from the breast and weaned from the milk. That sounds like a command to teach children the Bible as soon as they are done breastfeeding.

With so much time spent entertaining myself as a child, the Bible became what I read often. The stories of the Old Testament characters fascinated me. The fact that God was so intimately involved in the matters of his creation led to an obsessive-compulsive approach to study.

# THE CHATTAHOOCHEE RIVER, COLUMBUS, GEORGIA

This is the most profound river in my life by far. Reporting to Fort Benning for the first time in 1985, the Chattahoochee dominated the Fort Benning narrative. This mighty river would become home in my life no less than five times.

The Chattahoochee River has on its banks acres and acres of Georgia yellow pine. With pine trees come pine needles, and with pine needles come chiggers, a distinctly Georgia phenomenon. I will one day ask God the question "Why chiggers?"

Between 1985 and 1995, I would spend many nights in, over, or around the Chattahoochee River. I became an Airborne Ranger, and the river was my training ground. Good and bad things occurred along the Chattahoochee.

I would exit an aircraft in Airborne School after flying over the mighty Chattahoochee. Two years later as a Ranger team leader, the river would become the signal for one minute, as I was a student in Jumpmaster School.

That river would be my guide into Fryar Field and Lawson Army Airfield no less than sixty times. I have exited a C-130, a C-141, a C-5, a CH-47, a UH-1H, a UH-60, and an OV-10 Bronco, after departing Lawson Field and flying over the Chattahoochee River.

I have helo casted from a CH-47 and a UH-60 into the Chattahoochee on numerous occasions. I have performed a water jump into lake Eufaula, an Alabama tributary lake of the Chattahoochee.

The Third Battalion headquarters and my home of five years and three months was a mile and a half from engineer landing where so many pivotal events of my Ranger career occurred. The RIP barracks where I attended ROP were above the Chattahoochee River.

The first deer I ever killed was on Ley Field along the Chattahoochee River by Fryar Field where so many airborne operations occurred during my Ranger career. I cut my Ranger teeth in the swamps surrounding the mighty Chattahoochee.

I have paddled for miles up the river to depart for a live fire from the banks of this great river. RB7 watercraft are an amazing way to tour the Chattahoochee River, and no better team to do it with than B Company Third Platoon!

My roommate in B3/75 was E5P team leader Dan Busch from Baraboo, Wisconsin. He was an incredible Ranger who loved hunting, trapping, and fishing, and more than anything, he loved the world's Messiah, Jesus Christ. Dan was Christian. He did not just talk about it; he truly believed every word of the Bible.

I was an intemperate womanizer as a young Ranger away from home. Alcohol fueled many nights in bars where brass poles and naked women were everywhere. Dan never judged me! I would come back to the barracks blistered, and Dan Busch would be awake reading his Bible, praying for my salvation.

Dan welcomed me to the Third Battalion when most of the NCOs were skeptical whether I had what it takes, since I had never attended RIP and I became an NCO outside of the regimental model. I pray Dan's belief in me made me better and motivated me to succeed. No better Ranger mentor than Dan Busch!

Christian courage was a trait Dan Busch displayed in a Ranger unit where morality was a word quoted in the Ranger creed, without any tenet governing what is moral. Self-relevance on all questions regarding morality was accepted if the unit was not embarrassed.

Dan did not see it that way for his life. He was in love with one woman he intended to spend eternity with. His moral compass was no doubt learned from his incredibly virtuous mother, whom he loved. Dan was a family man through and through. His values are what set him apart as a man and as a Ranger.

If I only had the courage to believe what Dan believed, but that was not God's will for my life at that time. The seeds Dan planted in my early years as a Ranger leader are now bearing fruit in the lives of other Rangers returning from war.

Dan would teach me to navigate over long distances along the banks of the Chattahoochee River. He would share his dreams of attending selection and one day serving as a member of the unit at Fort Bragg. He would be married and take his bride with him on the life journey God had for Dan.

Any success I had as a Ranger is because Dan believed in humanity and he found a way to believe in me. Empathy is what Dan taught me. To know I was only as good as the least in my squad, and to understand I am no better or no worse off than anyone else, helped me in ground combat.

Dan taught me to respect the Rangers I was given the responsibility of getting ready for war. "Lead with led" was Dan's battle cry. He believed in our nation, and he believed in the Ranger creed. He taught me so many lessons I would need and lean on after returning from Somalia. I was changed as a human.

The seeds of leadership were first sown in my life by Dan Busch. I am indebted to so many more Rangers who made me better and frankly wrote my evaluation reports for me. I owe Dan and the Ranger regiment everything for accepting me and turning me into a man, even if it took a long time.

The last thing to occur along the Chattahoochee as a Ranger haunted me for a long time. First Sergeant Glenn Harris was my friend, a mentor, and an incredible Ranger leader. How he felt about our company was on display the night he died in Ranger service to our nation.

Glenn had finished his time as first sergeant of B Company. He had handed the reigns to Mark Nielson. Yet he chose to jump with the Ranger company he took to war. Why? Glenn loved the Rangers, and Somalia no doubt proved to him why.

The Chattahoochee claimed my friend Glenn after he chose to be the last man out of the C-130 tailgate jump over Lawson Field. Human error in training had taken an incredible combat-proven leader and a great man! Glenn, I will see you on the other side of glory.

Glenn and Dan shared a belief in our world's Messiah. Choose Jesus Christ and we will all see Glenn and Dan receive the soul winners' crown on the other side of the life equation.

RLTW
October 9, 2022

\*\*\*\*\*

In January 1990, I would report to Airborne School and rendezvous with the river that has profoundly impacted my existence. After two weeks of ground branch of the Airborne experience, my destiny was to view the river from above. My first five exits from an aircraft took place after crossing the Chattahoochee River, one minute from Fryar Field.

In February 1990, I reported to the Seventy-Fifth Ranger Regiment and had my first encounter with Staff Sergeant Sean T. Watson. When a noncommissioned officer desires to serve in the regiment, a three-week orientation and selection process is in order, which is called Ranger Orientation Program (ROP). I attended Ranger Orientation Program in 1990.

Different from Ranger Indoctrination program, which is attended by every candidate below the rank of E-4. ROP is a chance to see if the candidate indeed has the physical mettle and moral concupiscence to serve in the finest fighting fraternity on earth, the Seventy-Fifth Ranger Regiment.

Week 1 included a physical training test administered to determine if you make the minimum requirement to serve in the regiment. Fifty-two push-ups in two minutes. Sixty-two sit-ups in two minutes. Six pullups. And the two-mile run in under thirteen minutes and fifty-six seconds.

After the physical training test, classroom instruction on the history of the regiment back to the Revolutionary War was next. Basic patrolling and operations order, make-up of units in the regiment, and potential for combat deployment are all subjects covered in depth in ROP. Testing is at the end of week 1.

Week 2 was helicopter operations, airborne operations, and more physical training twice daily. Friday would be the twelve-mile road march, completed with a minimum of forty-five pounds in your rucksack and basic load of web gear and M16 rifle in under three hours.

The final hurdle in ROP was to exit an aircraft during daylight and darkness with the Ranger combat equipment that will be a part of your basic load should you be chosen to serve in the regiment. I would have the number 1 spot in the door from which to once again view the Chattahoochee River from the air.

After the jumps, our fates were decided. I would be assigned to the Third Battalion, Seventy-Fifth Ranger Regiment. I would report on Monday. I would proceed to the PAC office to see where the CSM would assign me

To my absolute delight, I was assigned to Weapons Platoon, Bravo Company, and another rendezvous. I was so excited to once again see my Ranger buddy Paul Mercer. This time, I was a young sergeant from another unit with zero real Ranger experience, and Paul fresh off his combat jump into Rio Hata, Panama.

My first day in Third Battalion saw me introduced to my new platoon mates. They all had combat scrolls on their right shoulder, with mustard stains on their Jump Wings accompanying their combat infantry badges. I had basic airborne wings, a Seventh Division Hourglass on my right shoulder, and a CIB issued for being a police officer in war.

That evening, it was decided I'd be taken to the platoon house of ill repute, the Pillow Talk Lounge (PTL). It was located on Broadway Avenue in downtown Columbus about 150 meters from the river. The area today has been totally gentrified by people who retire and settle in Columbus.

The PTL was legendary. To this day, I have never figured out if we were even allowed to be there. I think it was determined that illicit drug activity occurred there, so it may have been off-limits to Rangers. So much for the brigands' and hooligans' idea succeeding!

As we arrived, a few privates thought it good timing to begin doing shots of tequila. I bought in, and they drank water shots. I had three rather large young ladies dance on my lap for my first experience with how Weapons Platoon of Bravo Company viewed beauty in women. The bigger, the better.

As the evening progressed, I got more and more drunk at the expense of the men I would come to call my Ranger family over the next five years. When last call was announced, I had to be carried out of the lounge. I still do not remember the drive back to building 4832, and our home.

Around 0900, Tuesday morning, found me having missed my first formation in the Ranger battalion. As the door burst open, my platoon sergeant, Gene Potocki, began screaming at me to adorn the starch and spit uniform and report to the first sergeant. I knew my Ranger career ended as quickly as it had begun.

I report to the first sergeant. I am standing outside of his door with everyone laughing at me. As I report to hear my fate, the other three platoon sergeants start laughing about how big my testicles must be to miss my first formation as a leader. No sense blaming anyone; no one forced the liquor down my throat.

First Sergeant Chinn immediately took a disliking to my combat patch. No love lost between Seventh ID and the Third Ranger Battalion. It would take months, but eventually he cut my combat patch off after I received my EIB. He suggested it may be better for me to wear an EIB with no combat patch or CIB. I concurred.

This day saw my introduction to Sergeant First Class Carlton Dedrich. He was my first platoon sergeant. I would be assigned to room with Sergeant (Promotable) Dan Busch. This, more than any relationship I entered in the Rangers, changed my life forever. Dan would first introduce me to the Messiah he loved and treasured.

I lived about two miles from the Chattahoochee River while staying in the Third Battalion barracks. This river would be where I cut my teeth as a young Ranger leader who would one day be asked to come good on the Ranger creed. To all who have served in the regiment, the creed is our bond to each other and our nation.

I entered Bravo Company as a boy with a man's stripes on his lapel. By the time my life along the Chattahoochee ended during this chapter, I had been transformed into a lion ready to defend the freedoms this country promises its citizens. My introduction to Jesus Christ occurred two miles from Lawson Airfield and the river that had begun to shape my life.

November 10, 2022

# A RANGER'S RIVER

Life as an Airborne Ranger begins on Fort Benning, Georgia. Legends and leaders are born in the woods surrounding the Chattahoochee River. I served under, and with, men who epitomize the Ranger tenets taught in the Ranger battalion: courage, competence, candor, and commitment, rounded out by an incredible dose of common sense.

These are the attributes Rangers learn from their mentor's and heroes. I will attempt to describe the men who made me and the leadership they tried to instill in this intemperate womanizer with no moral compass. Ranger by day, hooligan by night and weekend.

Recognizing I volunteered as a Ranger, I fully knew the hazards of my chosen profession. The first sentence of the Ranger creed is recited by every member of the regiment every day of their Ranger career. I myself had no idea the dangers I would confront once I landed in a Ranger assault company.

As a member of Weapons Platoon with a military occupational specialty of mortarmen, my life revolved around supporting the three line platoons that would do the company bidding. I was the fire direction center chief who operated the mortar ballistic computer. When indirect fire was required, I did the math.

I learned the finer points of jumping on black top runways while practicing airfield seizure. Mortarmen carried basic Ranger load of ammunition for an M-16. They carried mortar rounds in their already overloaded rucksacks. I, additionally, carried the mortar ballistic computer. To exit an aircraft!

My first year would see me attend Jumpmaster School, Pathfinder School, Basic Noncommissioned Officer Course, and successfully passing the Expert Infantry Badge test, all while learn-

I began to believe in the Jesus of the Bible while disagreeing with every person in my life who adhered to the Catholic faith. The knowledge of my grandparents' Jewry led me to question why my parents eventually divorced.

I know now that it must have been confusing for my mother in my father's house during Christmas and Easter and at her parents' house during Passover and Hannukah. The Catholic church does not exactly have a great record in dealing with Jewry.

I wondered if anti-Semitism played a role in the demise of my parents' marriage.

Along the Delaware River, I learned the good and bad of religious ideology. I learned the hard lesson of just how far society has moved away from the truth of Bible morality, and I learned that the Catholic faith is anti-Semitic, anti-Christian, and not monotheistic.

When I was around ten years old, I opened the Bible to Daniel chapter 10. As I began to read, the Holy Spirit spoke to me for the first time in my young life. I was being called to be a watchman for America and to the nation of Israel. God had a perfect will for my life, and he was orchestrating my entire life.

I left Delaware county for good on September 23, 1987, when I reported to Fort Ord, California, for my first infantry assignment on active duty. I would visit home many times after joining the Army. Once I had returned from war as a Ranger, my path would never allow me to sojourn in the land of my nativity ever again.

I do not regret my childhood one bit. To honor my father and mother, today I teach every letter of scripture. Only the word of God can correct religious thinking and reveal the perfect, pleasing will of God for each of our lives. My early mistakes are my first great lessons from God.

*He was crucified upon a cross of wood, yet he*
*created the hill upon which it stood.*
*He is alive forevermore, and he is returning*
*for his virgin bride very soon.*

RLTW
October 8, 2022

ing the finer points of daily and weekly Ranger life. A thousand miles an hour would be an understatement. Fortune favors the bold! Lead with led!

After seven months in Weapons Platoon, I was recommended for the promotion board. With my MOS, this carried a penalty I was not willing to pay. There are only two E5 slots for 11C in a Ranger company, and I have two people with seniority ahead of me. I did not want to leave Bravo Company.

My friend and mentor Sergeant First Class Dedrich suggested I turn in a 4187 to change my MOS to 11B. My Ranger tab provided the justification for reclassification. I agreed. In April 1991, I would move to Third Platoon and begin my life as an Alpha team leader in a line squad. My first squad leader was Staff Sergeant Paul Holt.

He would be the first African American Ranger in a long line to help me as a young Ranger leader. At the time, in a company of 110 Rangers, only four were African American. All were incredibly able leaders and more competent leaders than I encountered in the regular Army.

I would begin to confront inherent prejudices learned in public education during my time in Paul Holt's squad. This pattern would continue as I served four more years in Third Battalion. God would place Max Mullin, Clement Green, John McGlothian, Hugh Roberts, Darrell Moore, Darren Smith, and many other African American leaders in my path that helped me overcome racism.

Second Squad, Third Platoon were a bunch of rabble rousers. I would be the Alpha team leader with Marc Belda as Bravo team leader. We had Aaron Weaver and David Eastabrook, with Steven Anderson who would last until 1993 and our deployment to Mogadishu, Somalia.

Paul Holt would be injured on an airfield jump onto North Field, South Carolina, three months after I first became Alpha team leader. Sergeant First Class Green decided to leave me in his job position at least temporarily. As it would have it, I would remain Second Squad leader until I took over Weapons Squad in September of 1992, with my promotion to staff sergeant.

Aaron Weaver and I would become good friends while serving in Second Squad. We would attend Sniper School as partners, and he ensured I would graduate. We would Jumpmaster together on no less than fifteen to twenty occasions over the next two years.

The men of Third Platoon were an incredible lot from all over United States and at least a few of Mexican descent. Most were poor White kids who joined the Army in search of upward mobility. The Rangers afforded the opportunity for them to see what their lives were made of.

Our platoon had incredible leaders. Bob Gallagher and Larry Moores would take us to Mogadishu and our date with Ranger destiny. The men they would lead had traveled the globe preparing to meet the enemies of American values and freedoms.

We measured our mettle in the swamps, creeks, and pine thickets surrounding the Chattahoochee River on Fort Benning, Georgia. The three years we would train in places most people know not exist provided the environment for overcoming fear and honing our skills as Rangers.

Friendships were forged through trial and tribulation. We experienced the full range of human emotion while learning to lead with led. Death in training, injuries that ended Ranger careers, and turnover make it a requirement to learn to appreciate all our team members who did not quit.

The Ranger platoon most often resembles a dysfunctional family when not killing the enemies of our nation. Relationships sometimes boil over from the sheer frustration of having no one else to fight.

When you absolutely, positively need something destroyed and burning in eighteen hours, the Rangers are who America sends. Third Platoon was where I learned that I am no better or no worse than any other Ranger in my Ranger family. The Ranger leadership model requires empathy learned in hardship!

I learned to endure starvation and sleep deprivation, and I learned just how wet a human could stay for long periods of time on the banks of the Chattahoochee River. Life was somehow more real for me as a Ranger.

I am old now. The young man who learned his trade alongside the greatest Americans ever produced now has only fading memories of those we would lose later in combat and most unfortunately to suicide. The Chattahoochee River provided waters of refreshing as I became a man in Bravo Company 3/75.

> *He was crucified upon a cross of wood, yet he*
> *created the hill upon which it stood.*
> *He is alive forevermore, and he is returning*
> *for his virgin bride very soon.*

November 10, 2022

# THE RIO CHAGRES,
# PANAMA

I reported to Fort Ord, California, on September 23, 1987, as an 11C Infantry mortarman, a private. Leaving reserve duty for HQ 1/9 Infantry Regiment meant I had to report to my active-duty unit at the rank at which I graduated advanced infantry training in 1986.

My squad leader was someone who aspired to a career in the Army. He made me the driver in an 81-mm mortar squad. I eventually became the platoon leaders' driver and eventually would drive for the regimental commander for a short period.

A healthy bit of competition began between my squad leader and I over physical fitness. He aspired to go to the Army Ranger School, and I wanted to ensure he was indeed ready. I knew not what a Ranger was; I just knew I was better than my squad leader at physical training.

Our first major deployment was to the republic of Panama to attend the Jungle Training School at Fort Sherman. Little did I know, I would be deployed to Panama three more times by 1989, culminating in my unit supporting the invasion in December of 1989.

In 1988 my squad leader was given the chance to take the pre-Ranger PT test and swim test administered by former members of the Ranger regiment serving as cadre on Fort Ord. He did not want the slot. The slot was to be lost for good, if I had not been so cocky.

I immediately expressed my desire to fill the slot and pass the PT test and swim test the following day. My platoon sergeant capitulated rather than lose the slot and face the embarrassment. In the morning, I would get my chance.

As I reported to Combat Leaders Course and the makeup PT test, I was greeted by Sergeant Jose Gordon. He would be my grader, and he would end up being a lifelong friend. He was a Grenada Raider from 1/75, and he would return there to again jump into combat in Operation Just Cause.

I would pass the PT test and the swim test to the disbelief of my entire chain of command. Now I had to put up or shut up. My time in the jungle of Panama and the Rio Chagres would serve me well those cold and rainy nights along the Yellow River in Florida phase of Ranger School.

I had no experience with the Ranger handbook. I had only ever been in units who relied on vehicles to transport them on the battlefield. My learning curve of everything Ranger would tend toward the extreme. I had a lot to learn in a very short time.

Combat Leaders Course saw me reunited with Sergeant Gordon. He would be my teacher and my grader. He understood I had more brawn than ability and I had zero experience in leadership positions. I was a private first class 11C who had never been in a patrol base. I had never heard of the five-paragraph OP order.

In the jungle, everything wants to eat you: from the tiniest flying insect, to the leaches, to the snakes and spiders, and even the ants if you stand still long enough. The humidity is awful always. The canopy does not allow sunlight to reach most places. Along the Rio Chagres, the mosquitos are bigger than helicopters.

Jungle training allowed for me to begin to confront any fears I may have learned along the way. The Rio Chagres was also where my lifelong obsession with all things God created took on new relevance. Learning to survive in a hostile jungle environment would serve me well throughout the rest of my life.

In CLC, I began to grasp the leadership model Ranger School begins to teach young aspiring soldiers. The challenges I would confront both physical and extremely mental sowed seeds that I carried with me when I eventually reported to Third Battalion in 1990.

The greatest impression was the leadership of Jose Gordon, who had served in the Ranger battalion. He took me under his wing, from my perspective. I admired his candor and his humor. It was the hardest thing I had attempted at this point in my life, and the Rio Chagres prepared me to confront the worst of it.

I graduated CLC with a recommendation that I be allowed to attend the Army Ranger School. My life was about to change in a very short time. I would spend the spring of 1989 preparing for Ranger class 11, with a reporting date to Fort Benning on June 1.

Our unit was deployed to Panama in April 1989. We pulled a rotation from Fort Smith guarding American interests and rehearsing one potential role our unit would take on if the hand of the president were forced and Noriega needed to be removed from power.

My last visit to the Rio Chagres would occur in May 1989 as our platoon crossed Gatun Locks in HMMWVs and headed into the jungle for one short stay and training mission. An encounter with bees cut our mission short.

The next time I would visit Panama would be on a combat deployment in support of the Ranger regiment who would seize two airfields as other forces took key sites within Panama. Our job was to enter the cities and stop any looting. We became military police officers as far as I could tell.

Nevertheless, I would reenlist during the invasion of Panama for the Seventy-Fifth Ranger Regiment unassigned. My reporting date to Ranger Orientation Program was February 1990. Some of my greatest military memories began in the republic of Panama along the Rio Chagres.

*He was crucified upon a cross of wood, yet he*
*created the hill upon which it stood.*
*He is alive forevermore, and he is returning*
*for his virgin bride very soon.*

RLTW
October 9, 2022

# THE YELLOW
# RIVER, FLORIDA

If I was to label this experience, this chapter may be titled "Boys to Men." To avoid copyright infringement for the name of a '90s boy band, I will stick with the river where this takes place.

Most civilians have never heard of this north Florida river. If you have, you probably know a Ranger who successfully learned leadership beginnings in the swamps and creeks that surround the beautiful Yellow River.

To get to Florida phase, this young wannabe would require incredible help from a source I now know to be God to get me through Darby phase and Mountain phase. The people whom God placed around me deserve all the credit for my successful graduation.

I reported to Fourth Ranger Training Battalion in early June in 1989. I was assigned to C Company. This was a heavily laden officer and cadet class. The Ranger training model required enlisted personnel be spread across the class. My squad was made up of a couple of battalion-enlisted personnel and a few other leg-enlisted people from the regular Army like me.

I knew the least about all things Ranger. I had graduated the Pre-Ranger Course, yet I had no idea after that. I loved Pt. I listened, and I could carry a heavy rucksack. I could easily starve and still perform physically. I had zero grasp of the Ranger operations order.

In my squad was Private First Class M203 grenadier Paul Mercer from B3/75 Ranger on Fort Benning. I had no idea how much our meeting in Ranger School would shape the next thirty-two years of our lives. Our friendship began in the first phase of Ranger School, at Camp Darby on Fort Benning in Columbus, Georgia.

I was really having trouble grasping the five-paragraph order and then applying it to patrolling tactics. I had never been in an infantry unit that walked everywhere with rucksacks. I was promoted to SP4 just prior to reporting to this school. I had never been required to formally lead men.

God placed Paul in my life to first get me through Ranger School. I have never questioned this. He had been raised in the Third Battalion, where leadership is required of every member of the regiment. His foundation would help me begin to grasp the truth behind what makes the Ranger.

After the order has been issued, commanders' intent is rehearsed, and problems are identified and solved; after one final rehearsal, it is time to patrol and complete the mission. There are three main missions taught in Ranger School: reconnaissance, movement to contact, and ambush.

Paul was not the reconnaissance type; neither am I. We loved shotting stuff, and we loved blowing stuff up. Luckily the patrols I would be required to lead were ambush and movement to contact. Paul would help me on every mission. I decided I would carry heavy stuff when he was in charge.

In Darby phase, I would begin to understand what it means to be hard. I would begin to learn that hard times do not last forever; hard men do! Blisters, exhaustion, and information overload would all plague me at Fort Benning. I failed my first and only patrol. I began to believe I would be recycled.

I would then be introduced to peer-evaluation reports that are part of every Ranger cycle. After the instruction is complete, the patrols are graded, then your peers tell you how they feel about you and your importance to the team. Little did I know, there was a system established long ago to weed out spotlighters who pass patrols, but then slack off when it is not their turn.

Somehow, Paul had decided I was worth something, and in Darby phase, I would receive my first peer evaluation, and because of Paul and the rest of the battalion guys in my squad, I would peer high enough to move on to Dahlonega and the mountains of north Georgia.

I carried my blisters through to Camp Merrill. The twelve-mile road march almost did me in. It was my peers who prodded me through as they introduced me to Ranger lingo. *Chow thieves, spotlight Rangers, leg,* and *buddy fucker* are all terms I began to master in Dahlonega.

I failed both patrols in the mountains. I did, however, begin to grasp what was required to move on. I carried a lot of weight to help guys pass their patrols. I volunteered as often as possible to help Rangers pass. This is how to adapt when you know you are not as good as those around you.

My peer evaluations would again carry me through mountains. I was now 0–3 on patrols. My Ranger instructor explained that I was so close to grasping the minimum requirements, the command was allowing me to proceed to Florida. A date with the Yellow River was on my horizon.

Ranger life got real for me in July 1989 and my rendezvous with East Bay Swamp: helicopter insertion, long-range patrolling in a swollen river basin and surrounding swamp, rope bridges, snakes, small boat operations, spiders, chiggers, extreme darkness, and even more extreme hunger and sleep deprivation. Not to mention being soaking wet for fourteen days.

I was called upon twice for graded patrols in Florida. The Yellow River is where Ranger truth became real. It was not the duress; it was the true human spirit. Paul Mercer ensured I made it through. I received a platoon sergeant go and a squad leader go on two tough missions, and it was my Ranger buddy Paul who ensured my success.

The Yellow River is where I cut my teeth as a new Ranger. The life lessons learned in Florida one summer month have served me well in my Christian faith.

Empathy is what Christianity was always supposed to teach. Rangers began to teach me to serve a cause greater than myself: I had to learn to serve others. I learned I was no better off or no worse off than the members of my Ranger team. I began to grasp the importance of having a true Ranger brother in the swamp surrounding the Yellow River.

I began to understand just what Jesus Christ was willing to do to ensure my success!

> *He was crucified upon a cross of wood, yet he*
> *created the hill upon which it stood.*
> *He is alive forevermore, and he is returning*
> *for his virgin bride very soon.*

October 12, 2022

# THE SCIOTO RIVER, SOUTHERN OHIO

After joining B3/75 in the spring of 1990, I met Staff Sergeant Richard Eugene Merritt. He was a squad leader in First Platoon. I was in Weapons Platoon. Rick and I spent a lot of time together between 1990 and 1995. We were roommates from the barracks to the home on Wynnton Road after Somalia.

When First Sergeant Chinn decided to leave for the CSM Academy, we received First Sergeant Darrell Moore. To say their leadership styles were different is not a judgment; I enjoyed both for the most part. Nonetheless, First Sergeant Moore would be injured on a jump, and BCO was introduced to First Sergeant Birddog Gambrel.

Our company was blessed with NCO leadership at the first-sergeant level down to the spec4 mafia. Dean Gambrel was different. He had a hilariously condescending humor that corrected thinking. He loved the Rangers and wanted to serve their cause. We laughed every day while doing our business.

We were deployed to 29 Palms for company live fire training. General Wayne Downing, our first regimental commander, and USSOCCOM commander at the time of our deployment, would be overhead viewing our maneuvers. Helicopter live fires add an incredible dimension to realistic when fast roping mixes with brownout and bullets.

The noise of the helicopter delivering four ranger squads from a thirty-foot hover. Sliding down ropes, while bullets are being fired in all directions takes incredible courage.

On this deployment, my platoon drew the fortune of being in the assembly area awaiting the turnaround of the birds to pick us up and insert our platoon. I knew something was wrong when the birds returned with people from First Platoon, who should still be on the objective.

Reports began to come across the headsets that a team leader from Second Platoon had been shot: Jeffrey Palmer. General Downing had his pilots land the bird to try to get him to the hospital. Jeff would die en route. An accident in training had claimed a Ranger's life.

I do not remember anything about the end of that exercise. The next memories I have are of myself, Rick, and First Sergeant Gambrel, with most of Bravo Company on a bus, headed to Pennsylvania to escort our brother's remains to his family. Then on to Arlington to bury a Ranger team leader.

Rick and I decided we would spend our upcoming leave at his home in Lucasville, Ohio. This would be my introduction to the Merritt family and the mighty Scioto River. I would participate in squirrel hunting for my first time; now I spend months training tree dogs.

I would visit the Southern Ohio Correctional Facility where Rick's brother, Ralph Jr., worked. I would win a dance contest in the town of Portsmouth. But most importantly, I would meet a truly virtuous woman. This story is part of a redeeming time in my life. Sandy Merritt alone changed my thinking about relationships!

It was 1991, the days between Thanksgiving and Christmas. It would be the second Thanksgiving and first anniversary of Rick deployed to Panama while the family watched their younger brother, JD, succumb to cancer. The Merritts were grieving.

Rick learned of his brother's passing the day after Third Battalion jumped into Panama. Sergeant First Class Dedrich shared the story of how he wept as he delivered the news on Rio Hata, at Rick's blocking position. The soldier in me learned a lot about what was expected of me as a Ranger leader.

Rick had every right to leave Panama. His legend began on this date in Ranger history. Staff Sergeant Merritt would never leave his men behind in combat. I found Rick in the Bible. He is Uriah the

Hittite. The most loyal soldier I have ever met, he accepted both the good and the bad of the profession.

Rick's mother, Sandy, I found in Proverbs 31. She is the virtuous woman identified by King Solomon, and it was Sandy who was the epitome of what I thought a Christian woman looked like. She became one of my life's heroes, and I would not realize it while on top of the mountain in my Ranger career.

It was only in the greatest valley I ever faced in life did I begin to recognize why God placed Sandy in my life. She would begin to teach me relationship to a partner that revolved around mutual respect and grounded in the agape love of Jesus Christ.

My relationship to Rick Merritt really began in Scioto County, Ohio. It has continued for thirty-two-plus years now, and I pray that our best days are ahead. Rick has stuck with me when I probably would not stick with myself. He has supported me when I did not deserve his support.

His mother, Sandy, unabashedly loved Jesus Christ, adored her husband, and raised her boys to be men and her daughter to womanhood. She is the greatest female example I have ever had in my Christian walk. I cannot wait to greet her on the other side of glory as she receives the soul winner's crown for teaching me Christian faith.

The Scioto River has had a profound impact on my entire life. After visiting a prison, I would end up incarcerated. Yet still, the Merritt family never judged me. They, in fact, prayed only for me to meet the Jesus they loved.

I learned to hunt on the Scioto River, and now I hunt squirrels and hoggs along the Obed and New River corridors of Morgan County, Tennessee, my home until the Lord calls me home. Come meet Betsy Ross, my black mouth cur female who loves getting after things.

So many seeds were planted in my life that have served me well during my sanctifying years of Bible study. The Scioto River and the Merritt family deserve so much credit for where I am today as a man and as a Ranger. In Christ's service, JB.

# JOHN BURNS

*He was crucified upon a cross of wood, yet he
created the hill upon which it stood.
He is alive forevermore, and he is returning
for his virgin bride very soon.*

November 11, 2022

# A RETURN TO
# RANGER COUNTRY

January 1992 would bring renewed vigor to Bravo Company. Out training cycle was hard and compressed: continental deployments; battalion, company, and platoon external evaluations; and two more training deaths. In-between, I would attend five schools.

Rick had moved to the Ranger Indoctrination Program to evaluate candidates for service in the regiment. I was Second Squad leader, Third Platoon. Our first test would be at Fort Chafee, Arkansas, and the evaluation of our unit at the Joint Readiness Training Center.

We had a new platoon leader in Johnathan McGlothian. He was an African American West Point graduate. I admire him for accepting the challenge of being a platoon leader in an Airborne Ranger Rifle Platoon. The pressures on officers to succeed are immense.

Two reactions can occur when a new platoon leader appears. He will either micromanage, or he will become intimately attached to the platoon, and the men he has have been given an incredible chance to prepare for war.

One way leads to insecurities and fear of failure; the latter leads to your men writing your successful Officer Evaluation Report that will guarantee advancement and promotion. Some allow themselves to not trust anyone outside their own ability, and some trust those who have gone before.

This is very important to grasp about Ranger leadership. Bullets will one day be exchanged, and I would rather obey someone that trusts me more than they fear me! Ranger leadership ability is best learned by those who have the humility to learn from those who have done the bidding!

The year 1992 would see the first Ranger Hall of Fame class inducted. It would occur on the heels of a regimental mass tactical airborne operation and the first Ranger Rendezvous. The friendships begun at Rendezvous 1992 have grown and lasted a long time.

The names speak for themselves. The men I met are Ranger legends. I pray that when it was our chance to engage the enemies of freedom, we have made these American heroes proud.

Their names are Colonel Ralph Puckett, Dave Maddog Dolby, Bull Dawson, Terry Roderick, Smokey Wells, Pat Tadina, Wayne Mitsch, Bill Bullen, and so many more Ranger legends.

I believe a man can never determine where he is going until he confronts and understands where his ancestors have been. Ranger ancestry continues to remind America that Ranger families are birthed in the fires of armed conflict between men who just do not agree.

Rangers' success is dependent upon the lessons learned in warfare by our predecessors. To understand how their success and failures are teaching tools can keep us alive in war. This is an amazing testament to the respect Rangers have for all those who have gone before us. Thank you, Ranger brothers, for showing me what was expected of me!

I was promoted to staff sergeant in April of 1992. My time as second squad leader came to an end as I assumed responsibility for the Platoon Weapons Squad. I would be deployed to war with these American Ranger heroes, but not before enduring many trials and even many more all-night parties.

Machine guns rightly discerned require an understanding of the physis of ballistics. When friendly forces are counting on you to provide fire from an overwatch position, the flight of bullets being fired in the cyclic rate of fire need guidance to place effective fire and not have fratricide incidents.

Life got serious for me as Weapons Squad leader. I was blessed with three highly competent gunners in Dominic, Chris, and Kasey. Their assistant gunners and ammo bearers were no less competent or important: Dave, Tim, Dominic, Sandy, Reese, Chad, and Jason. All would be deployed to Somalia, some with even greater responsibility.

I was chosen to attend Malaysian Survival School in September 1992. My roommate, Dee, had successfully completed the school and told me it was an awesome experience. I pray my friend has had an incredibly prosperous life. We had a good time together as young Ranger squad leaders.

I completed the task in Malaysia and returned to the banks of the Chattahoochee, freshly motivated by Ranger success and ready to face our upcoming challenges as a competent Ranger platoon. Little did I know that 1992 would end the same way for Bravo Company, as did 1991.

My first day back from overseas, I went to the mess hall after PT with my squad. I spoke with other squad leaders about my journey. I recommended each one travel to Thailand at least once in their life as soldiers.

The battalion commander, John Kenneally, approached me as I stood at attention. He told me "At ease" and asked if he could join us. He congratulated me on my accomplishment and then asked that I report to his office that evening; he wanted to discuss something.

Certain men have influenced me in ways I did not grasp while it was occurring, none more than John Kenneally. He was a Ranger through and through. To be a Ranger battalion commander, a certain degree of empathy is required. I feel he oozed with this godly trait.

As I reported to his office about 1945 hours, he was packing his gear. I saluted, and he told me to please have a seat. His next question secured his legacy as the greatest commander I ever had. And there were many great ones.

He asked me if I, and my men, had everything we needed if the president were to call upon us. Twenty-one Ranger line squads of nine men each and nine weapons squads, and he is asking about mine! That is a Ranger leadership example.

We proceeded to share young men's pleasantries as I asked where he was headed. Little did I know, this night would be his last on earth trapped in this flesh. He was headed to Utah to evaluate First Battalion Commander Lieutenant Colonel Stauss and the men of First Ranger Battalion.

Legends were lost on that fateful Utah flight: John, Lieutenant Colonel Stauss, Harvey Moore, the pilots, and the crew. And another

Ranger legend was present to attempt a rescue of the downed aircraft: Doc Donavan.

So many lives changed, and the worst was yet to come as Third Battalion received the news.

Ron Russell assembled the battalion. He taught me another very valuable life lesson: It is okay to cry as Rangers. We lost family. I look to my faith, which Colonel Kenneally shared. I look to his final leadership challenge found written in his tombstone in Arlington: "It is not the destination that matters. It is the journey you take along the way."

Rangers need each other. Our profession affects us like no other. Peace after war, most days are nothing more than a stubbornly persistent illusion. We are a DNA family forged in war and peace. It is a blood family we Rangers claim, which can never be denied.

RLTW
November 12, 2022

I will see John Kenneally on the other side of glory as he receives the soul winner's crown for placing this Ranger's feet solidly upon a path leading to the mercy and grace of Jesus Christ. Until we meet again!

## Ranger Proving Grounds

The year 1993 would turn out to be the most interesting year of my life. I was enjoying my time as Weapons Squad leader. I had completed schools furthering my education in the Ranger profession I had chosen. I had incredible leaders and even more incredible squad members.

I was living in a three-bedroom home with Rick and Dee. We had been introduced to some new female companions who were aspiring students at Auburn University. The friendships I made in spring of 1993 have proven to be timeless. Was the fun time a reprieve from God before the greatest trial of my life?

Rick was teaching Ranger Indoctrination Program, after competing in Best Ranger in 1992 with Kurt Buchta. They won the most important event as Rangers, the moving target range. They completed the competition with an admirable midtable finish.

Now, Rick and I decided maybe we would give it a go. We began training in earnest in February. Rick was completely focused on the task at hand. I, on the other hand, was completely focused on something new for me: actually having a relationship with a girl that lasted more than a weekend.

As we approached the competition, we decided to internally evaluate our self-readiness. Teams were decided on readiness. I was nursing an ankle sprain from practicing the spot jump from a helicopter. I did poorly on the internal road march. Rick and I mutually decided it was better that he compete with Josh Sherry, who was much more prepared.

I would be partnered with a young corporal from Alpha Company. Two young Alpha Company NCOs would be the best chances for success from Third Battalion. Our primary teams would perform admirably while coming short of victory. I and my partner did not complete our task.

While training for Best Ranger, I would be introduced to a former Third Battalion member living in Columbus who had a monetary investment in the local Gold's Gym. This meeting would come to be a harbinger of the troubles I would incur after returning from Somalia.

Bravo Company was busy traveling the globe. As I returned to normal duty hours, my squad members were returning from a training deployment to Thailand. The battalion had already taken part in a jump into Korea that year. Next stop: Fort Bliss, Texas. Our rendezvous with destiny!

Summer was spent enjoying physical training with a squad who could all outrun me. To recognize this truth is what made me always try harder to beat them. I used it as an opportunity to make us all better. Rick and I continued road marching to the barbershop and the bars on Victory Drive.

We made several excursions to Panama City Beach for some much-needed rest and relaxation. Our platoon was getting tight. Without knowing it, we were on the brink of becoming a fam-

# JOHN BURNS

ily. Sometimes dysfunctional, always loyal! Never shall I fail my comrades.

We arrived in Texas to begin training with the other branches of Joint Special Operations Command to rehearse missions we may indeed be called upon to spearhead. It was July 1993. I was having the time of my life.

I finally found a family on earth I could totally be myself in that was holding me accountable every day. The microscope of other Ranger platoon members watching your every move keeps Ranger leaders competent. The spec4 mafia governed the Ranger assault company!

In Texas, our focus shifted to helicopter raids performed at the company level. Our platoon would also be called upon to test an idea born out of war. We would attempt to drop a bulldozer out of a C-130 and have Rangers chase it over the tailgate. Yes, I said that!

Our jump altitude would be increased, and I would be asked to be the jumpmaster. After successful insertion jumps under fire in Grenada and Panama, the need for a bulldozer was a logical solution to solve the problem of obstacles on an enemy runway, designed to slow the Ranger assault.

As a practical physics equation, I have the gift of hindsight. Imagine a bird not using the bathroom for six years, and then releasing the matter instantaneously while trying to control the waste's descent and landing. Never mind the speed at which the bird will need to climb to avoid losing thrust after depositing an object that is incredibly heavy and moving forward at 125 mph.

Then introduce Airborne Rangers willing to exit immediately after the bulldozer is released. We would test this theory through practical application with live jumpers. Hooah!

Let's cut to the chase. As the aircraft approached our drop zone, a drone parachute was deployed. The bulldozer would clear the tailgate as the pilot hit maximum thrust, and we pitched near vertical. We, happy band of Airborne Ranger brothers, left the aircraft as a shotgun round.

We trolled. No one was standing as we all were thrust out of the aircraft almost simultaneously. My parachute risers had the greatest twists of my career jumping. Luckily, someone much smarter than me understood the physic of inertia.

I gained control of my parachute as my thoughts turned to retrieving the bulldozer and actually starting it. I figured if this worked, the regiment would develop a new skill with a new identifier on the end of my MOS: *11b3vB4F7 Bulldozer Operator.*

It was not meant to be. After running the two nautical miles required to locate the bulldozer, I was astonished to find it in a vertical position with the blade about six feet below terra firma. A giant caterpillar lawn dart!

Luckily, we were Rangers. We learn from mistakes. The only thing left now was to rig another bulldozer and try it again Friday. Rangers lead the way!

November 13, 2022

## A Prelude to Peace

It is no coincidence that in the latest iteration of men and women returning from war, we find the allies of peace and those who propose a perpetual state of warfare would begin to bicker over the need for a standing military.

Those who profited most from war now seem to believe their utopian ideas can deliver world peace. On the contrary, for capitalism to survive and thrive, poor people must be called upon to wage warfare to ensure the dollar remains the world's reserve currency.

The people who themselves have never fired a shot in anger control every aspect of the returning warriors' lives. They offer free education in hopes we will fall prey to the dumbing down of the American society in the public education system through university.

Indoctrination has replaced education. The free exchange of information Thomas Jefferson aspired to instill in America has been hijacked by those willing to offer only Greek, eugenic models for their Darwinian high society. These people find peace counterintuitive.

Freedom has a price the protected rarely understand and are almost never willing to pay!

Greek and Roman thinking has delivered on a sociopolitical elite class of educated eugenicists willing to apply their knowledge gained at university to remain in power and control the flow of what they alone consider an education.

In university, a prospective student is offered electives to include mythology. All mythology is included, except the one that I happen to ascribe to. You can enjoy learning the Greek mythologies, the Persian mythologies, the Muslim mythologies, even Christian mythologies at university, but never Hebrew mythology. Only the Hebrew Bible has been outlawed in public education. Why?

Israelology, the study of the nation and the people we call Hebrews. Today they make up the Jewish population found as a prosperous community in every nation on earth. I happen to be descended from these ancient people.

Their mythology book is the Bible. It has its roots competing with great empires. The real estate it occupies today is the most contested space in human history. Kings have waged war to plunder it. Religious zealots have shed blood for thousands of years over Jerusalem, the ancient capital of the Hebrews.

Today, every nation on earth has united to stop this smallest minority on earth from prospering. Yet every geopolitical decision being contemplated revolves around and directly impacts the nation of Israel, nowhere more than America.

As America returns from the twenty-year protracted war on terror, which will not end until Jesus Christ is on his throne in Jerusalem, we better buckle our seat belts. The enemies of Israel and America are now being freely allowed to emigrate here. War will reach our American homeland very soon.

Our best warriors are still killing terrorists in the Middle East. The military at home is concerned with advancing social issues and purging the ranks of all those they consider insurrectionists. I fear our military cannot rescue the Jews from the coming persecutions that will occur when the American dollar collapses.

I fear Americans will not be able to recognize despotism. I fear our children are being indoctrinated and not educated to deal with coming world events. I believe that government in any form exists for only one purpose: to create a manufactured crisis. Get our entertainment and news industry to control the narrative: fearmonger their way into Americans' minds to increase budgets that deal with the crisis they originally manufactured; shift wealth from those who have it to those who do not, then spread the money out to political organizations, where money can then be funneled and, dare I say, laundered into community activism, which again sows more chaos.

Power is what they all crave and we are becoming more powerless as a nation and both parties designed it that way.

Noah was a conspiracy theorist. And then it rained.

Science knows this. World mythologies have left clues modern archaeologists refuse to understand. God has raised up poor folks in camouflage and overalls with common sense. These folks believe the Bible!

I am one of these deplorables. We have no political leanings for we are devout monarchists. We believe in a coming king and kingdom centered in Jerusalem. We believe in one God having three distinct persons. We believe this God is the sole creator of the universe.

I believe a man can only receive peace in this life by turning to the creator who can actually deliver peace.

That creator is the manufacturer of the most preposterous debt payment plan in human history. His yoke is completely easy, and his burden is light. Harness yourself to the burden bearer of creation.

I shared my testimony about Mogadishu, Somalia, in my first book, *Behind the Veil*. It was a coming-home experience to write the book that led to a series of seven. I was instructed by God to share my shortcomings from the journal I kept after coming home from war injured externally and internally.

To find peace, I had to confront warfare. My experiences in war led to the hamster-in-the-cage syndrome. I had the ability to get on that stupid wheel and go round and round, accomplishing nothing. Something had changed in my internal wiring.

I became hopelessly lost, and my attachment to my Ranger brothers faded. Addiction to all things narcotic followed, and the endgame for me was incarceration in a federal prison camp for six months. That experience would save my life.

I suggest listening to someone who has waged war in any quest you may be on to find peace. I offer my perspective based upon my own experience in failure trying to find peace on the lonely road that leads to destruction.

This book is the only method I have to try and help others not make decisions I made after doing exactly what my Ranger creed expected of me in war! It is what I promised my nation and its citizens in my enlistment oath, which I took on no less than three occasions.

Finding peace nowadays is about identifying my Ranger brothers contemplating the loss of joy in this life. Focusing on their lives helps both of us find peace after prosecuting war.

I pray our nation will listen to us old warriors freely offer pragmatic problem solving and sound leadership advice. My prayers point to the Messiah suspended between heaven and earth, offering his hand in marriage for eternity.

November 13, 2022

## A Time of War

August 1993 saw the battalion being deployed to Texas to begin rehearsals, for a contingency being considered at the national command level. B3/75 would join the regiment to support JSOC planning and rehearsals.

Our platoon would practice closed-quarter battle drills, helicopter insertions, and airfield seizure operations. Our platoon was the company jump-clearing platoon. We would be called upon to jump on a runway and clear the subsequent runway to prepare for follow-on forces.

We would test the ability to use jump platforms to deliver earth-moving equipment.

The mission we were rehearsing would not be the one that affected JSOC in the Global War on Terror.

Our company was alerted in August 1993 and flown to Fort Bragg, North Carolina. The beginnings of Task Force Ranger were being gathered from the four winds to begin rehearsing a mission to Mogadishu, Somalia. I did not even know where it was on the map.

Planning and training would begin in earnest. The original Ranger package was to include a platoon from Alpha 3/75 supporting the Bravo Company helicopter assault package. They would be readied to adopt and drive HMMWVs in urban terrain.

We would train for about a week and a half. The president had not made a deployment decision; this was just rehearsal. We would return to Texas to resume training with the rest of the Seventy-Fifth Ranger Regiment, now assembled at Fort Bliss, Texas.

Two of our NCOs requested a pass while in El Paso to visit family. Lorenzo Ruiz requested that Marc Luhman accompany him to visit his mother and daughter. Sergeant First Class Gallagher approved an overnight visit. Off to El Paso, Texas, these Ranger brothers would go.

At around two-thirty the next morning, Bravo Company was alerted and told to prepare for a deployment to Fort Bragg to rehearse the mission to Somalia, while the JSOC command and the National Command Authority wrestled with the size of the deployment package.

For the first time in my Ranger career, the words *rules of engagement* and *rules of war* were being thrown around by people not going to be in our task force. This was counterintuitive to the "Lead with led" narrative I had been taught by Killer Man's Sons for three-and-a-half years.

Nonetheless, our task force was tailored to accomplish how the powers that be saw as able. We would now be called upon to support our own task force internally. Third Platoon assumed responsibility for driving the HMMWVs, and the mission package began to practice after being tailored.

Alpha 3/75 would be cut from the package. AC-130 gunships would be scratched and redeployed from supporting the current mission to Mogadishu occurring as we prepared to deploy. Amazing. Send in the pro team, and then take away their trump card should a violent firefight break out while operating.

This would serve as a harbinger of things to come for Task Force Ranger.

We would be deployed in late August. America was sending the tip of the spear into the lion's den. Rude men would now do the bidding of well-educated politicians to stem the flow of radical Islam into the West.

Violence would eventually be required, and the president would prove he did not have the stomach for it. Maybe it is time we get a warrior who served in the White House? Someone who respects the poor people they send to secure the US dollar to keep them in power? When will America learn?

We accepted our role in Somalia. Third Platoon would be required to provide blocking force protection at strong points chosen during planning. We would be responsible for task force resupply. We would share the responsibility for guarding the compound with the rest of B Company.

We were constantly rolling in the outskirts of the city where men would soon be required to prove the Ranger creed. Danger was around every corner as we settled in; the reconnaissance and intelligence people took over, locating our prospective targets.

Mortars would fall in the grass surrounding the helicopter's position close to our billeting area. We would fill thousands of sandbags as we struggled to protect the thin-skinned helicopters from fragmentation. The party started immediately for Task Force Ranger.

We would travel to Sword Base, where the United Nation's quick reaction force, now manned by units from the Tenth Mountain Division, were. Another harbinger for TFR. These young infantrymen would take part in the Battle of the Black Sea, and they would perform heroically.

Our platoon would cross train with some of their engineers in advanced demolitions in urban environments. We would keep the task force resupplied by traveling to bases strewn across Mogadishu. We would support every mission during our deployment to Somalia. This would take a toll.

Lieutenant Moores would lead us in deploying eight HMMWVs in combat. We would be supplemented by heavy weapons, and members of internal Weapons Platoon would prove to be more than capable of operating. Danger was the lot for every member of Third Platoon and Task Force Ranger.

In warfare, it helps to have really funny people to entertain America's finest. Our platoon was gifted with the incredible humor of Dominic Pilla. He started a satirical cartoon he would draw and then supply verbiage to highlight something the chain of command did that was "STUPID."

He would have willing participants he outranked gather and rehearse skits to entertain the task force when we were not busy. These skits were funny. Dominic lightened our load while doing really serious things for America.

My time in war was not always chaotic. I choose today to focus on what united my brothers and I to accomplish an incredibly complex American Special Operations mission. My Ranger brothers experienced the range of human emotion. Young men were required to perform amazingly.

October 3, 1993, would see another Ranger unit secure an eternal legacy in warfare. I would lose nineteen family members. I would lose many more Ranger brothers to suicide since returning from Mogadishu. America would lose many more Ranger brothers of mine in war.

I pray America ponders what they ask young, mostly poor Americans to do for all of us. I know the cost of freedom. It must be continuously repaid from generation to generation. It is never earned by birth!

*He was crucified upon a cross of wood, yet he*
*created the hill upon which it stood.*
*He is alive forevermore, and he is returning*
*for his virgin bride very soon.*

November 15, 2022

# THE NILE RIVER, ETHIOPIA

The geopolitical impact Ethiopia had on our deployment to Somalia has never been highlighted. We found ourselves referees between two competing ideas about civilization: the Ethiopian Christian model and the radical Islamic model of Sharia in Mogadishu.

Ethiopia had been plagued by encroachment of Islamic ideas: Sudan to the south and west, Egypt to the north, the border with Somalia to the south, and a long-running civil war in Eritrea over control of shipping. Religion was at the center of every decision.

Somalia relied on the seasonal rains to supply water to the Nile tributaries that flowed south into Somalia. Ethiopia and Egypt require electricity in huge amounts. A decision was reached between the two nations to build a new hydroelectric dam along the southern edge of the White Nile.

The effect this decision had on the people of Somalia can never be overlooked. Government decided that Somalia was not as important as rapidly growing Ethiopia and Egypt. Severe drought in the late '80s and '90s led to the rise of Islamic fascism as tribal Muslims defended their own water sources.

The people of Somalia had settled in to twelve basic families. Islam was not a priority for most regular Somalis trying to survive without food or water. A charismatic Somali army general began to hijack food and water supplies coming from the United Nations.

In 1992, an American contractor who had previously served in US Special Mission Units was ambushed and killed. Larry Freedman was Jewish. He loved America and Israel. He served in every conflict including Vietnam.

44

He was a founding member of Delta Force. Now, a Somali warlord had ordered Americans ambushed and killed. Larry would succumb to his injuries. Men he had served with were now commanding our task force. I believe his memory drove decisions in planning our missions.

I believe the Somali people wore their Islam lightly on their sleeves. Family, food, and water were their priorities. Only the radical group of Muslim men behind the Habr Gadr clan made it their priority to keep America from succeeding. The fight for freedom had reached Mogadishu.

Muhammad Farah Aydid was the leader of the largest clan, strictly because of his ruthless policy of hijacking food supplies and then blackmailing other Somali clans before killing them one clan at a time. By 1993, only two tribes remained since civil war broke out.

We would enjoy limited support from the rival faction to General Aydid and his Habr Gadr militia. The Abgal clan was hanging on in their fight for survival. Problem is, I do not know if their ideas were our ideas.

It was convenient for them to stay on the sidelines and let us get rid of Aydid and his leadership team. We would do the killing, and they would restore peace when the radicals had been eliminated. Finding anyone truly loyal to the Somali government proved most frustrating.

Task Force Ranger would be caught in the middle of a family feud and a religious war. Neither side truly trusted us, and neither side had the UN vision for what eventual peace in Somalia looked like.

Did I mention that after the collapse of the Soviet Union, Mogadishu had become the world's largest outdoor gun market? Russian generals defected and sold their weapons in masse. Corruption plagued any government America aspired to install in Mogadishu. Russia pretended to support the UN.

Italy also had a contingent of peacekeepers stationed in the area occupied by the people we were chasing. Intelligence had assessed that the Italians had become complicit in hiding Aydid and his command infrastructure from the pursuit of the UN peacekeeping force.

Myself and Aaron Weaver would be called upon to drive to their compound and escort an intelligence officer to discuss options we hoped they would consider. Their arrogance would end in the Italians tucking tail, packing up, and leaving Somalia. Now we could freely operate without UN interference.

While parked inside the gate of the Italian command compound, I believed Aydid entered the complex right before our eyes. The Italians were adamant about us not keeping our weapons loaded.

As a suspicious vehicle entered the place, the Italians yelled for them to get out of here, that the Americans were here looking for the general. To this day, I still believe it was General Aydid who was thirty feet away, and we could do nothing.

We alerted TFR headquarters as they scrambled a recce bird to track the suspicious vehicle. Rangers did their job. Time had allowed for an escape, and the wrong vehicle was tracked to a suspicious house across town.

The ground assault force launched, and we raided the home of the man in the white vehicle the recce bird tracked. We were successful in arresting the police chief who supported us. Intelligence was gathered, as I was questioned about the surety of my sighting.

My men agreed that the man we saw closely resembled the general we were hunting. The man we arrested was not the man we saw. The wrong vehicle was tracked, no one was injured, and Somalia now knew we meant business. I counted it as a successful Ranger lesson in courage.

This was the beginning of the journey our platoon took to Mogadishu, Somalia, in the summer of 1993. Warfare was real, and the Ranger creed echoed in all our minds. The mission to capture Aydid and his men had begun with a successful rehearsal mission without casualties.

My two vehicle teams would take part in five more successful raids. On three missions, our platoon would be fired upon and return fire with minimal casualties. Young Rangers began to prove why the regiment is the best infantry force known to man.

Nighttime was the right time for operations in Somalia. Our success may have contributed to the decision-making that went in to our daylight raid preparations on October 3. Our success contributed directly to the decision to conduct a daylight precision raid.

Many men would call out to God as bullets, bombs, and rockets saturated the roads we were fighting to stay alive upon. Now we all would be required to come good on the Ranger creed.

November 15, 2022

## Mogadishu, Somalia
## Summer of 1993

I was deployed to Somalia with the Ranger company I had cut my teeth with. The men who came before me had voices that echoed in my head. My time as an innocent, unproven Ranger had come to a close.

Time to come good on my enlistment oath and, more importantly, see if I am the man in the Ranger creed. Now more than ever, I would be a pawn to evaluate whether the Ranger leadership model, adopted by the regiment in 1984, was working.

The mission package adopted for deployment would be missing one trump card from above, the AC-130 Specter gunship. This platform alone gives Rangers a direct fire platform, with no vulnerabilities, for the Somalis possessed no antiaircraft weapons that could reach five thousand feet above ground level.

The mission was accepted by our task force commanders. Every unit would take part in the planning, the rehearsals, and the eventual execution of the mission. The foundations forged in Fort Bragg would grow upon our arrival in the Mog as we began to settle in and prepare for missions.

The hangar became our home. Rodents were dealt with accordingly when the best shooters in the world possess 22 LR rounds and firearms. We shared a common billeting area: common shower area, common weight room, and mess hall. We lived among giants.

Our cots were segregated only by elements. We mingled among our mentors. They took part in our Ranger humor and taught us a few things that could keep us alive. The best thing for me was my reunion with my hero, Daniel Busch, now an operator.

Truth is, Dan and I were like kids together when we spent time alone in Mogadishu. Dan was serious about three things: his relationship to Jesus Christ, his love for his wife Tracy and their new baby boy, and his desire to serve his nation as a premier Special Forces soldier.

Task Force Ranger grew into an effective fighting force. What was hard to overcome was the understanding of individual unit TOE structures. The Green guys are the best shooters, movers, and communicators on earth. The Ranger TO&E required a little more central leadership role.

We gained some individual sovereignty in my platoon. We had the vehicle mission in Somalia. This allowed for more time traveling at the platoon level through dangerous parts of the city. I believe it helped our drivers on October 3, when it really mattered.

I look back on my time in Mogadishu; God finally allowed me to understand my life unto that point in time. My leadership style was one where I understood that most Rangers assigned to my squad were better than me at most tasks. I had to show up every day to earn their respect.

Rangers would rather follow someone they respect a lot more than they enjoy following someone they fear. The regiment has a model for soldiering that cannot be duplicated. The microscope is your men. They watch every move and decision made, to be scrutinized by the spec4 mafia at the earliest convenience. From private to colonel, the standard is the same. To grasp that you are only as good as the weakest person in the squad leads to an empathetic view of leadership.

The Ranger platoon is like an internal combustion engine. Valves, bearings, rods, seats, and chains all make up the engine. This holds true in a Ranger platoon. Privates, specialists, corporals, sergeants, staff sergeants, a platoon sergeant, and a platoon leader—all are needed for success.

There were three rifle squads under the control of a staff sergeant. He has two team leader sergeants, who in turn have one pri-

vate first class rifleman, one saw gunner, and one grenade launcher/
rifleman making up each fire team. This constitutes the Ranger rifle
squad.

The machine gun squad supports the three rifle squads. A staff
sergeant oversees three gunners (each usually Ranger School grad-
uates and usually the rank of corporal or specialist), three assistant
machine gunners (specialists or private first classes), and three private
first class ammunition bearers.

The Ranger platoon has a radio telephone operator from within
the platoon, a platoon medic, a platoon fire support noncommissioned officer, and his RTO. On occasion in Mogadishu, we were
augmented with Air Force Combat Controllers or an extra task force
senior medic.

A better understanding of Ranger TO&E would have enabled
planners to recognize a requirement for more rehearsals dealing with
catastrophic instances as would be encountered in the Battle of the
Black Sea.

The greatest obstacle encountered after the bullets started flying was inflexibility from certain leaders within our task force to
fully comprehend what made our ideas about fighting different. Yet
we still managed to overcome incredible odds to live to fight another
day.

Leadership is a principle. It revolves around getting others
to accomplish your mission by providing them with a purpose, a
direction, and the motivation to overcome whatever they encounter
between where they are at and the finish line of success. Flexibility is
an inherent quality.

The Rangers had one abiding principle taught to us by men
who took part in this firefight: Lead with led!

To harness war fighters to rules justifying conduct in war is
completely counterintuitive to success in gunfights. Rangers accepted
the challenge of deployment to Mogadishu as part of the JV team.
We were there to support our older brothers in Task Force Green. I
am glad we lived among each other.

The confidence to overcome was evident to Rangers as we witnessed the extreme might of the American military apparatus. We

were being mentored by the greatest warriors on earth. We lived among the men who would show us motivation on a scale I never witnessed.

Through it all, I feel Rangers showed America and our task force leaders why Rangers gained the mantra "Rangers lead the way!"

I pray our dead have received mercy and grace from a God who continues to shed his grace on those who accept the challenge to defend America.

I pray our wounded have recovered and moved on to productive lives, fulfilling their dreams.

I pray the survivors would continue to honor our fallen by sharing this story whenever they get the chance. TFR was the greatest experience of my Life. I became a man on the streets of Mogadishu.

I learned that Jesus Christ was indeed who he said he was, as I learned true Christian empathy while serving a cause greater than myself as a Ranger Weapons Squad leader in combat.

*He was crucified upon a cross of wood, yet he*
*created the hill upon which it stood.*
*He is alive forevermore, and he is returning*
*for his virgin bride very soon.*

November 19, 2022

# THE POTOMAC RIVER

My flight home from Mogadishu was much different than my flight over to Africa.

The flight over contained the best fighting force America had assembled since Vietnam. Five hundred of the healthiest warriors in service to the president made the journey into the Mog. Now, I was wounded and traveling on a C-141 transport, with wounded Rangers stacked to the ceiling like cordwood.

No branch of service was spared. My litter shared space with wounded operators, a severely wounded Navy SEAL, wounded Air Force Combat Controllers, and wounded Army aviators. No rank was spared: from private to sergeant major, from lieutenant to lieutenant colonel. The injured soldiers came from every background.

Our destination was home, America—land of the free, because of the brave. The price of freedom became real to me once again as my freedom flight home would begin the long process of recovery I still am struggling with today.

My physical injuries remind me every day how America finds heroes from places in our land most Americans have never heard of. I was now flying to Germany for stabilization surgery, before being shipped to Walter Reed Army Medical Center.

My thoughts were on my brothers in the task force who now had to shift focus and concentrate on finding our dead and missing family members. These men were strangers in August when this journey began. Now, we are blood relatives forged in the crucible of ground combat.

War is intimate. Bullets know no boundaries. In Mogadishu, my biggest life lesson has caused me to question certain things about society. Some men died with little training. Some men died with a

51

modest amount of training. Others died with an unlimited access to the means to prepare for war. Men die in war!

In this war, the men were my family. Now I had to focus on their plight. They were in Somalia. Their brothers left in body bags and on stretchers. Now they had to complete the Ranger mission. I was now in relative comfort at a military hospital in Germany.

Innocence in my life was now gone. I had taken human life. I had witnessed men I came to respect cry out to God as their final breath left them. I had brothers that were incredibly maimed. Adrenaline had carried me through a four-hour ordeal, never rivaled in my life again. I was changed.

My life flashed before my eyes no less than four times on October 3, 1993. Processing all I had witnessed would prove to be the greatest challenge I would face. How I accepted Mogadishu definitively ordered my footsteps for the next twenty-nine years and counting.

Death had presented itself to me. I feel the normal thing would be to question "Why did I survive and men so much better than me did not?" I had the added dimension of my leadership role, and men I had prepared for war were now dead. I began to question why I existed.

The Potomac River provided the backdrop for me to finally visit the Capitol and the Smithsonian Museum by myself. The nation's capital was where my renewed vigor to understand America began anew. I began to realize our entire social system is built upon utopian views on eugenics.

Our government exists to control every aspect of the governed person's existence. From our enrollment in public education from pre-K to university, thought is what government desires to control most. Only the view of radicals is accepted as educational, and our entire system is guilty.

It was in DC that I began to question my own morality. The Ranger creed required I remain morally straight. Would I choose the government model of alternate families, rewards for promiscuity, legislation of homosexuality, and transgenderism as human rights? The murder of the human genome in the convenient altar of the womb of the woman? Cowards calling themselves men?

Delusion was manifesting in our country, and if fighting in war was to amount to anything for me, I had to adopt the tenet of Dan Busch to guide my newfound desire for absolute morality. From this time forward, the Bible alone would be my guide, and the promised Holy Spirit alone would be my teacher.

What did it for me were the funerals of my brothers buried in Arlington being broadcast on every channel in Walter Reed Hospital. I saw Deanna Joyce and was reminded of Kasey. An aspiring young couple. Kasey's dreams evaporated after a Somali bullet felled this heroic Ranger.

I looked into his pale face for fifty minutes. I owed him my testimony to accept the Jesus Christ he believed wholly in.

I owed Dan Busch my sincere attempt to understand the Jesus Christ of the Bible narrative. It required me to first shed any care for what men think. I would only care what God thinks from now on. My journey into the truths of the Bible began in earnest in 1993.

First thing I began to question was, why is the Bible the only book the government feared enough to legislate out of the American education experience? It shocked me that two famous Catholic brothers did this after seizing the power for the social democrat party birthed under FDR.

A new view of society emerged because of two Supreme Court decisions, both based on radical interpretations of the Constitution and Bill of Rights. Their entire suit would evaporate today based solely on the knowledge of vocabulary and history.

The Danbury Baptists gave us the separation of church and state as a request to Thomas Jefferson, not our laws. Removing prayer and the Bible from children's lives angered God, and the Kennedys received a double portion curse still playing out in their family successors' lines.

Questioning a nation's mythology has led to my believing in the greatest mythology ever accepted as true by men. It is the Hebrew version of mythology found in both Testaments of the Holy Bible.

Our presidents have sworn to defend us while holding their hands on the Bible they had no intention of believing in!

Only Jesus Christ will one day deliver the utopia men seek!

November 20, 2022

# A Ranger Family Reunion

In November 1993, about twelve days from my twenty-sixth birthday, I was notified that I would be traveling to Fort Benning for the Bravo Company Awards ceremony for feats of heroism. I would be flying home to Columbus and rendezvous with my Ranger family.

I was taken by ambulance to a waiting military transport airplane bound for Columbus, Georgia. A van greeted myself and a couple other BCO wounded able to travel back to B Company.

As the van entered our Ranger compound outside building 4832, the entire company was standing in formation. As we exited the van, our brothers broke ranks to greet us and welcome us home. Many of us had not seen each other since the morning of October 3.

After greeting First Platoon and my Ranger brother Sean T. Watson, I moved on to Third Platoon. I had not seen the members of my squad since my medical evacuation from Mogadishu. We had much to discuss. It was amazing to be back in the platoon area, minus two amazing Ranger leaders.

Dominic Pilla was my primary machine gunner assigned to Staff Sergeant Jeff Struecker's HMMWV in Mogadishu. Lorenzo Ruiz was my number 2 on my HMMWV.

We had a terrible day. From my position on the ground assault convoy, the events of October 3 unfurled before my eyes like a flag. I saw many men shot, blown up, maimed, and heroic all at the same time. The day was won by Rangers doing what Rangers do.

The Ranger leadership model worked. When a staff sergeant or sergeant was wounded, the specialists and private first classes moved up the leadership ladder of responsibility. I was most proud of the members of my platoon. Five of the six Ranger KIAs occurred on the ground assault convoy.

On my HMMWV, Specialist Ritchie was wounded early by small arms fire. My primary gunner, Clay Othic, was wounded in the turret engaging the enemy with his .50-caliber machine gun. Clay would find another ride on the five-ton truck being driven by Richard Kowalewski.

Lorenzo would take over for Clay. No hesitation from this warrior from El Paso, Texas. Sergeant Ruiz was fearless in life. He saved many lives with precision fire from the turret. A bullet fired from the roof of a two-story building would fall Lorenzo. Sergeant Weaver killed the Somali gunman.

I was wounded slightly by a single piece of hot shrapnel after communicating with Staff Sergeant Dave Wilson as he was blown up. I was shot in my left scapula when Lorenzo was hit. My third injury and worst gunshot wound would come as I looked down on Kasey Joyce's face as we engaged an enemy ambush.

My medic, John Stansfield, was most heroic after being knocked semiconscious by a bullet to his helmet.

As he awoke almost immediately, he went back to work, treating at first Clay, and later Lorenzo. John was a borrowed medic from Alpha Company. God saved John for a purpose. I later learned that he was a believer in Jesus Christ. I knew immediately why I am alive.

I witnessed Corporal Jim Cavaco get hit in the turret in the vehicle to my immediate front. He was killed instantly by a Somali bullet. The worst was still yet to come.

I would run past the stretcher carrying Kasey as the Task Force Green medic pronounced him dead. He would be loaded onto the cargo HMMWV for transport back to our base. The truck would end up disabled and abandoned as we were rescued by my platoon leader, Larry Moores, and his relief convoy.

On that HMMWV were two other wounded Rangers and the body of Sergeant Joyce, the wounded SEAL Howard Wasdin, two other SEALs, and members of Matt Eversmann's squad trying to reorganize at crash site 1. Thank God he had Specialist Dave Diemer and Private First Class Jason Moores.

These two young Rangers kept us in the fight. They engaged enemy targets constantly as we meandered our way home on flat tires and an engine about to explode. These young Rangers were heroes!

I would be cross-loaded onto a five-ton truck now being driven by a more-experienced operator from Task Force Green. On that truck were the Somali prisoners from the original target building.

Many had been injured or killed by bullets aimed at our Rangers on board.

I was seated across from Master Sergeant Tim Griz Martin. He had been blown up while seated behind Adalberto Rodriguez on two MK 19 ammunition cans. An enemy rocket-propelled grenade had breached the thin-skinned vehicle and detonated the ammunition sympathetically.

Both men were launched airborne with severe injuries. Master Sergeant Martin had lost his legs. He was still trying to organize Rangers to defend the truck. He was seated next to the mangled Specialist Rodriguez.

The worst situation was Private First Class Kowalewski. He had a live rocket-propelled grenade lodged in his torso, and his arm was severed. He was dead. The RPG was fired from so close it never armed. Now we were riding home under fire with this added drama.

I had witnessed Super 61 assume an orbit above my initial blocking position. I watched as the helicopter frantically tried to rotate its fuselage to give the gunners a chance to engage the RPG gunner who would knock it out of the sky. Dan Busch was on that bird.

I spoke with my platoon sergeant moments after he himself was shot in his hand. Bob was still cool under pressure as he sent me back to my vehicle with the instruction of disseminating to all what the current plan was. We had just driven past crash site 1 for the first of three times.

This is what we discuss as a platoon, but not this night. Tonight, we would party and go visit our favorite place to view girls hardly dressed. Tonight, we would honor our dead and wounded brothers by throwing down Third Platoon, Bravo Company–style.

I was glad to be home. I was changed. I just did not realize to what extent the change affected my judgment as an Airborne Ranger combat veteran.

November 23, 2022

# 1994

The year 1993 ended in tragedy on a scale not experienced in regimental history. Six Rangers from one Ranger company killed on a combat mission. Forty-one rangers from Bravo Company wounded. Three years running in my life, where Rangers paid the ultimate price for our freedom as Americans.

I was twenty-six years young. I had been to war, twice. I had a choice to make: continue serving as a Ranger or leave military service to find out what all the freedom I was fighting for is about. My ideas about freedom would prove to be unhealthy.

I was operated on in November. Dr. Heekin, an orthopedic surgeon, agreed to assume control of my healing process. My goal was to be off the military profile list to reenlist for another six years. A bone graft and nerve graft were needed to restore motion in my left leg.

I had saved some money while injured. I had never owned my own new car. I decided to take five grand and place a down payment on a Canary yellow and black Convertible Mustang GT. I ordered a five speed without thinking completely through my left leg injury.

My answer to the problem was to find a girl to drive me everywhere I needed to go. I put less miles on my own car than the girls I befriended while attending college at UCLA. To Rangers: University of Columbus alongside the airport. To civilians: Columbus State University.

My education experience in university began like most college students. Alcohol and sex made class attendance easy. I found university education as lacking and not at all challenging. I figure my experience in war had tainted my ability to understand peace.

I began to sleep on a couch in a home rented by no less than five or six Rangers in the Wynnton Road area of Columbus. The house was huge. Motorcycles fit easily in the living room. The number of women who stayed at that house can never be numbered. We were young men home from war.

I had too much time off! I had been accountable to my men and my platoon sergeant for six years of Army service since leaving home. Now, I only reported to John Burns. This is the beginning of the unraveling of a Ranger career.

I had begun to work out at the local Gold's Gym. My Ranger buddies were still training for war. The party never stopped in 1994. I decided to include anabolic steroids in my recovery process. Problem number 1 is, they are completely illegal without a doctor's prescription.

In the summer of 1994, I concocted a plan to travel to Poland, via Germany, to purchase steroids in quantity at a cheap price. I enlisted a civilian friend who was Polish to aid my travel. He introduced me to his brother who could purchase the product and pack it for transport.

My brain had stopped worrying about consequences. It was as if I was in the Army on paper alone. John Burns needed the structure of the Ranger platoon. Given too much time, a little money, and my brain will start figuring out how to come closest to the edge of challenging social rules.

I began flying to Germany monthly, renting a car in Frankfurt, and traveling over the Polish border in the town of Oder. I would meet my connection, load the package, and return to my hotel in Frankfurt and await my flight in two days.

This occurred three times. The money I made furnished Rangers with unlimited party favors. I even paid Rangers' rents when they struggled on an Army salary. The road goes on forever, and the party never ends! Thank you, Mr. Robert Earl Keen.

While attending college, I somehow made the promotion list for sergeant first class. It was my first time in the secondary zone of promotion. I had six-and-a-half years on active duty. I never believed I would make this list at this time in my life.

I wanted to return to being a Ranger squad leader first. Nevertheless, the Army decided I was worth promoting. Next stop, the Noncommissioned Officer Academy and a date with ANCOC. This is a requirement for promotion to sergeant first class.

My college experience ended in August of 1994. In September, the promotion list was published, and my platoon sergeant, Rick Merritt, decided I should attend ANCOC as a walk on. I was still on a physical profile, and I had not run two feet since October 3, 1993, when I was wounded.

I reported to ANCOC and received an alternate slot. I would share the classroom with Staff Sergeant Jim Pippen and Staff Sergeant Todd Hibbs, both men who would achieve great things in their own respective careers.

First, I had to inventory equipment and assume responsibility for the Special Skills Shop at Third Battalion. I was now assigned to HQ company. The veil of comfort and hiding on Third Platoons' roster was over. I would attend ANCOC with a graduation date of December 1994.

While attending ANCOC, I appeared on the levy roster for Vicenza, Italy. I know now that the CSM had decided I should take my Ranger leadership abilities to another unit; I did not agree. No use arguing. I wondered if this was not a setup for my steroid business I thought no one knew about.

My reporting date would be July 1995. I would pass ANCOC, but not before tragedy struck Bravo Company for the fourth year running. My heart would be broken, and it would take the next twenty-six years to begin healing. I would lose another mentor and friend to a Ranger training accident.

December 1994 would again not be a merry Christmas or a happy new year.

November 24, 2022

## How Many Have to Die

I had managed to meander my way to a passing grade through twelve weeks of the Advanced Noncommissioned Officer Course. The only requirement remaining for my successful graduation would be the final exam. It was December 1994.

While I studied and prepared to graduate, Bravo Company was preparing for a change of leadership at the first-sergeant level. Mark Nielson would be taking over from my friend and mentor, Glenn Harris.

I had been a young Ranger squad leader when Glenn first reported to First Platoon to assume the control of a team of Rangers that had been led in war by the legend, Carlton Dedrich. Little did First Platoon know, this would be the beginning of an incredible blessing from God.

Glenn was incredibly sarcastic. It made him really funny. He had a way of answering that caused you to question yourself. I had the luxury of being in Third Platoon; being Glenn's friend was possible without fraternization being a problem. B3/75 were family first!

Glenn had a beautiful wife and two healthy young daughters who would become part of the BCO family. Sandy, Tara, and Heather would grace us with their presence in peace and war. Sandy is a strong, courageous woman. She is an amazing leader in her own right.

Glenn would lead First Platoon through the trials and tribulations of Ranger platoon life. Only his promotion to E8 would take him away early. His success would lead to the appointment of another giant to lead First Platoon, Sean T. Watson, another incredibly talented leader.

A bus crash on the way home from Kilo 22 Range claimed the life of Toby John Young. His last name was befitting of his incredibly youthful smile. Glenn would be the calming force aiding Dean Gambrel as we said goodbye to another Ranger in a training accident.

Our company was becoming far too comfortable saying goodbye to teammates and brothers. We were a family. Getting over family death is never easy. Thank God we had Glenn Harris, who had faith in the God of the Bible, to comfort his Ranger brothers.

I never heard a word proceed from Glenn's mouth that was not encouraging. He gave everyone the benefit of doubt but demanded a high standard of honesty in leadership. If you were wrong, Glenn expected you to realize it before he had to get involved. Humility guided my friend Glenn.

Glenn would leave BCO for a short time as he had to serve as the S2 before he could become our first sergeant. The Army requirements meant there was always a Ranger waiting with seniority to assume control of the most coveted position as a Ranger assault company: first sergeant.

By 1993, Glenn was back in Bravo Company, and now he was our first sergeant. I was completely renewed in my motivation and desire. My friend and mentor was now home in BCO. We would begin preparing for war in earnest in July 1993.

Our deployment to Mogadishu galvanized the unit under the leadership of Glenn Harris. His motivation and devotion to Rangers would prove unequaled in my short Ranger career. While in Somalia, he supported me when I needed it most.

Glenn epitomized what it means to serve a cause greater than himself. His family had sacrificed so much to get him to this point in his Ranger career, and we were thankful for their amazing support and service. Glenn and Sandy were the model deployment couple.

While Glenn ensured we had all we need to succeed in combat, Sandy worked overtime to ensure the Ranger wives and girlfriends at home had all the information she possessed. She would raise her daughters to understand the meaning of selfless service.

This is the regimental model for husbands, as well as wives and children. We must never forget the sacrifices made by Ranger family members in peace and war. They make things right, and they complete the Ranger DNA family sequence. Inseparable!

The Ranger first sergeant is daddy of the Ranger company. He is the person responsible for keeping the unit prepared and ready to execute orders. His motivation becomes the company's motivation. His acceptance of risk sets the tone for all Rangers.

Glen accepted every risk in combat with the same vigor that he approached leading our company in peace. He was physically fit, mentally alert, and incredibly, morally straight. He is my Ranger daddy.

Glenn's time in Bravo Company came to an end once again because of his successes. He was added to the promotion list for CSM, and to get promoted, he would attend the Sergeants Major Academy. He would be departing Bravo Company bound for El Paso and a rendezvous with history.

Glenn had taken us to war from the comforts of Fort Bliss in the summer of 1993. El Paso, Texas, had significance to Glenn and Bravo Company. It was not in God's plans for Glenn. His time in the flesh had come to an end. God wanted him in heaven.

His change of concern would take place while Bravo Company was training for an airfield seizure mission on Lawson Army Airfield, on the banks of the Chattahoochee River. He had decided one more company mission was needed.

He did not need to be there. Yet still, Glenn jumped. He loved the men of Bravo Company. The only way to say goodbye was to lead them one more time. This is Ranger leadership on display.

An accident with station keeping equipment led to four men landing in the river. Three were recovered unharmed, while Glenn was missing. It was the night before my ANCOC final exam. I was summoned from the academy at 3:00 a.m. to come open the boat shop.

I met Lieutenant Wrieden, who explained that a jumper was missing in the river and it was Glenn. My life changed forever with his words, but for now, we had a search mission to assist.

I would return to the academy and take the exam early. I made it back to engineer landing as the news broke that Glenn had been recovered and he was deceased. I have spent the next twenty-nine years finding out about the sovereignty of God and his plans for our lives.

Glenn's dreams would become my dreams.

*He was crucified upon a cross of wood, yet he*
*created the hill upon which it stood.*
*He is alive forevermore, and he is returning*
*for his virgin bride very soon.*

November 24, 2022

# THE PO RIVER,
# VICENZA, ITALY

The year 1995 would begin the same way my previous four years began: Third Ranger Battalion trying to recover from tragedy and loss. To understand the effect my service in B3/75 had on my mental ability to find peace after prosecuting war has, most days, been nothing more than a stubbornly persistent illusion.

Larry Bernard, Roy Brown, Robbie Knight, Steven Palmer, John Kenneally, Dominic Pilla, Lorenzo Ruiz, Kasey Joyce, Jamie Smith, Jim Cavaco, Richard Kowalewski, Dan Busch, and Glenn Harris, Toby John Young—know their names. These men are my Ranger brothers who died serving the American idea of freedom.

Your freedom debt has been paid by American Rangers in peace and warfare. Third Ranger Battalion, in the 1990s and beyond, had proven that being a Ranger held real and present dangers. Freedom has a price the protected rarely grasp or understand.

This is not a statement of arrogance. Rangers serve at the behest of the president. They sign up for a profession that cannot be fully grasped, until service in the Seventy-Fifth Ranger Regiment becomes reality. I had no idea what I was getting into, yet I loved this profession more than any other in my life.

I had left home in 1987 in search of a little upward mobility. I was raised by proud ancestors who served in every war America had fought in the twentieth century. The American dream constantly seemed elusive coming from a family that worked hard. The military had become my home.

I had recovered from my wounds and had begun running again in October 1994—exactly eleven months since returning from

Mogadishu, injured to be precise. By January 1995, I had taken on the added dimension of preparing for marriage and an overseas duty assignment.

My new wife would be accompanying me on my assignment to Vicenza, Italy. I would be traveling by myself in May, and she would come over once I had found housing on the Italian economy. Arriving in Italy with a plan to serve as a platoon sergeant and then attend selection gave me renewed Ranger purpose.

I signed in to the battalion, after being picked up at the airport by a PSG from Alpha 3/325 PIR. There was a position coming open for Third Platoon, and he invited me to their yearly ball being held Friday evening.

After my interview with the CSM, he decided to assign me to the S3 office. Alpha Company First Sergeant Atkins intervened. I would serve as Weapons Squad leader for one month and then take Third Platoon. I would meet my new platoon members at the ball on Friday evening.

I had not fully grasped the effect my combat service meant to men who only ever played pretend war.

I wore my dress blues to the ball, and the questions about my combat infantry badge, BSMV, and Purple Heart began in earnest. I was a twenty-seven-year-old, two-time combat veteran, with seven years in the service, and the young soldiers I was assuming command of were ready to learn.

Mondays through Fridays would be spent training for war, Ranger-style. I had a young company commander in Mike Iacobucci, who understood the regiment that made me who I was as a leader. His trust and support led to our platoon successes immediately.

The battalion planned a helicopter drop outside Aviano Air Base. I was current in my qualifications to run a helicopter drop zone. I was summoned to battalion headquarters and the S3 to be briefed on my upcoming TDY trip and my need for a qualified driver from the platoon.

My choice of driver led to a lifetime of friendship. Ryan Edwards would drive me on the upcoming trip. We would be leaving in the morning. Uniform was BDUs: boots, berets, and civilian clothes for three days. Equipment would be one DZSTL kit from the battalion and golf clubs.

Specialist Edwards would learn a lot about Ranger Burns's ideas of team building. I believed in training hard for war. Only because I believed in partying harder in peace. The road goes on forever, and the party never ends!

The drop was uneventful and a success. My golf game was nowhere near Ryan's, but nonetheless, he became very important to me when I returned to leading men. The platoon I had inherited were losing in the motivation game. Time to increase standards by being an example.

Our battalion was given a training contingency mission to support UN objectives in Bosnia. Three things became evident: Helicopters would be our method of insertion, our objective was an urban environment, and our platoon would be in danger.

I had spent the five previous years preparing for this moment. My Ranger mentors' faces appeared in my dreams as I prepared the platoon for war. I began to teach demolitions at the behest of Captain Mike Iacobucci. The company was motivated as training intensified in Grafenwöhr, Germany.

We left Aviano Air Base and did an airborne insertion into Hoenffel's. On the drop zone was Brigadier General Dave Grange, my former Ranger regimental commander.

He saw my combat scroll and called me over for a reunion. The last time he had seen me was leaving the medical evacuation aircraft in Washington, DC. It was great to let him know I was back in the fight.

He alerted me to the fact that this mission was serious and that there was a great chance President Clinton would sign the deployment order. I had now been told this three times, and the previous two times it occurred. I had a job to do getting these men's game faces on.

The platoon achieved success, and we were certified, ready to conduct our mission. A return to Vicenza on a long bus ride was in order. Awaiting our platoon at home was a long weekend. Awaiting me was a date with a Criminal Investigation Division investigator.

My involvement with anabolic steroids had caught up with me. I would now be required to answer questions, and this time, my wife would also be questioned. I was not someone geared to tell on myself. A date with the polygraph led to my admission of guilt.

I did, however, refuse to tell if anyone currently serving in the regiment were involved. Fact is, I devised this plan all by myself. Yes, there are people I served with who knew what I was doing. They played no role in my guilt, and the bucks always stopped with me.

CID wanted me to tell on people who had nothing to do with my operation. I was also charged with lying because I refused to implicate others. Criminal Investigation Divisions prove constantly that they will commit a crime to catch others in guilt.

My time in the Army was over. I had made E7 in seven years, and now I made E1 in ten minutes! I was discharged from military service with an other than honorable (OTH) discharge, with the loss of all military benefits. I would be home in America in four days. The Army discharged me with the quote "No Longer Needed by The Service."

My wife and I would move to Palm Beach Gardens, Florida, and rendezvous with my Ranger buddy and Somalia veteran, Tim Bone Moynihan.

*He was crucified upon a cross of wood, yet he*
*created the hill upon which it stood.*
*He is alive forevermore, and he is returning*
*for his virgin bride very soon.*

RLTW
November 27, 2022

# ST. JOHN'S RIVER, FLORIDA

Time to find out what freedom looks like. I had been more than willing to defend it while never understanding what American freedom exactly is. What causes humans to leave their own countries bound for America? What did I fight for in my own terms? I never asked myself this question.

While I was in the military, the uniform code of military justice was the tenet that governed my life for seven years. Now the Constitution and Bill of Rights governed my behavior. These documents form the foundation of the American criminal justice system.

Federal law trumps state law. Do American laws produce more freedom? With America being the fourteenth largest population of developing countries, why does America incarcerate eighty-seven percent of the world's inmates? Does the law protect us? Who does it protect us from?

Our country is experiencing growth pains. The two-party system has only produced chaos and dissent. The income gap has increased exponentially. A middle class is a myth created by rich men desiring absolute control over every aspect of Americans lives.

The Constitution was conceived by sociopolitical elite men who practiced syncretism. They mixed a little bit of the Bible, with a whole lot of positive eugenics. Our founding mythology discounts two hundred years of well-established Puritan and Jewish history in America.

You cannot draft the Declaration of Independence without visiting the Quakers, Puritans, and Jews of New England. They believed in the Bible as the foundation of civilization. They believed in the family unit being the most important building block to achieve empire status.

They did not own slaves. Slaves were brought here first by the Spanish monarchy, which itself was eugenic in favor of Roman Catholicism. It is inherently a conquest religion. They, more than any, combine a little bit of pious Jesus with a whole lot of Babylonian mysticism.

Spain brought slaves here to St. Augustine long before the British monarchy established the slave trade in Jamestown, Virginia. God sent a storm that blew Mayflower off its course headed for Jamestown. Two competing ideas!

Monarchy produced the men who gave us the Constitution. These were elitist men, with titles held over in their ancestral history. The Puritans and Jews of Jamestown had ideas about becoming a shining city on a hill. That hill was Calvary. The city was Jerusalem.

Their Bible governed ideas about cohabitation with indigenous peoples. Indentured servitude is biblical; slavery is not! To indenture oneself to a cause greater than yourself without pay is God's model. Slavery without compensation is a monarchial idea carried out by eugenic-minded elitist men.

These men owned slaves. They built the slavery model in the South. Therefore, God emigrated true Christians into the South.

Southern heritage is not slavery. It is biblical Christianity. The soldiers who fought in the Confederate Army did not own slaves. Some leaders owned slaves, but not the common Jew or Christian.

In fact, the formation on the Ku Klux Klan came about after Southern soldiers were stripped of their federal right to vote after being paroled. Southern men played no part in the election and subsequent reelection of Ulysses S. Grant. The KKK was a minstrel show, until hijacked by the Southern Democratic Party that emerged after the war. These men were Baptists, not Christians! These racist men supported the Northern banks, who emerged victorious after the war.

No poor person won the war. The same bankers who prosecuted the war for the North control many aspects of the two-party system today. I am a different kind of monarchist. I believe in a coming Jewish king named Jesus Christ.

The two-party system has enslaved Americans to an idea that has atrophied over time. Separation of church and state has been hijacked by elitist millionaires who need not God in their lives. Where does that leave the rest of us?

One choice: Send our children to schools where only their ideas about education are advanced. History is rewritten in favor of the eugenic party in charge. We have all been fleeced of our wealth and taxes.

Only one way of thinking that is controlled by a class of people that never pay for their own fuel or groceries is tolerated. They are controlled by incredibly powerful bodies of immoral lobbyists. Money is their god, and power is their master.

Freedom to me is based upon true biblical insurrection. Neither party has my God's intentions in mind. Israel has been used as a pawn in every geopolitical decision made by these elitists. Their decisions are now affecting us in ways that only the Bible saw coming!

I was living on the intercoastal waterway as part of the lower St. John's system. I began to turn to the pages of the Bible for instructions on finding peace. I found only warfare. This warfare was spiritual, not external: a war being waged against myself, by myself. It held the key to my life.

I had to leave my ancestors' view of religion and freedom in the rearview mirror of my existence if I was ever going to rightly divide the word of God. The Moynihans were incredibly patient as they allowed myself and my new bride to live in their home. I am incredibly grateful to this amazing family.

Irony would have it that I would proceed to the unemployment office to claim what benefits I could without an income. What I found was an opportunity. Carpenters' apprentices were needed.

I proceeded to the local union hall to take an exam. I passed and started my new job on Monday morning with CR Wilson Construction. I would apply for and receive my GI Bill benefits after visiting a Florida vet center.

My first period of service, which was honorable, enabled me to apply for service-connected disability. It would take a year. I used my GI Bill to attend the apprenticeship training center for one and a half years. I eventually ended up working for Donald Trump at his resort in Mar-a-Lago.

RLTW
November 27, 2022

## Redeem the Time

Three words that have driven the last twenty-one years of my life. It is a command of God through Paul that ends the book of Colossians. What exactly is redeeming the time?

According to the Bible, God exists outside of how humans experience time. We exist in ten special dimensions, on a two-dimensional plane. Only PhD physicists and five-year-old children understand the true dimensionality of our existence.

The Bible rightly divided proves it was conceived entirely outside of how I exist in the vacuum of human time. In the beginning was the word, and the word was with God, and the word was God. This is an abject lesson in human time and God time.

In the beginning, God created the heavens and the earth. If you spend a lifetime studying creation from a pragmatic evidence-based perspective, this statement should become the basis for who you believe was on the cross.

This should also begin to make you realize just what the creator was willing to do to redeem his creation. God's thoughts are never man's thoughts. God is not trapped in the linear equation humans reckon as time. He is completely outside of time itself as sole creator!

If I was to ever understand God's ideas about redeeming time, every presupposition about God had to melt away. I had to leave my ancestors' versions of faith in the dustbin of my existence. I turned to the journal I began keeping and the prayers I wrote down.

As God began to answer all of the prayers that lined up with his will, the more I began to realize Christianity has nothing to do with corporate worship or doctrines of men. The Bible began to reveal that every day in human history was perceived by God in eternity past.

I began to realize I was reading a script for the greatest love drama ever conceived. I realized a war for my soul was indeed going on, and the church has no idea how to fight because they only wield one edge of the two-edged sword, that Jesus Christ refers to as the written word of God.

The redeeming of time began in earnest in my life as my wife and I returned to Columbus, Georgia, after eighteen months in Florida. I had only ever been an Airborne Ranger in Columbus. I had no idea how many traps the shining one set for me in order to make sure time stood still!

I had received a 70 percent rating from the VA, after it was adjudicated that my time in Somalia was under honorable conditions. My period of other-than-honorable service was March 1995–November 1995. God had begun to redeem the time in my life with the restoration of what I earned in war.

I had begun going to the VA for treatment of residual pain, and they determined sleep deprivation must be a result of post-traumatic stress disorder. Narcotics were prescribed, and once again, the addict sleeping inside me woke up.

It was easy to blame addiction on my injuries. This idea plagued me for the next eighteen years of my life. If a narcotic would make me sleep or numb the natural feelings of loss based on the number of brothers I have buried, I swallowed, smoked, injected, or drank it.

I had an incredible stronghold reigning in my members. Nothing human doctors suggested or prescribed was treating what was wrong inside my own brain. I was experiencing stinking thinking, and only a reprogramming by the creator of the universe would work.

He had to get my complete attention. While working at Mar-a-Lago, the federal government served me with a warrant for my arrest for the illegal importation of anabolic steroids; to wit, 2,600 dollars' worth. Now they were willing to upend the life I was beginning to get back because I did not report the income!

We returned to Columbus to face a judge. To add insult to injury, they were charging my wife for helping me. We showed up in court to have the charges read, and the ninety-three-year-old federal judge needed to be educated on what a steroid was.

I could not afford an attorney, so one was appointed for my wife and me. He would inform us that the evidence they were using was my own admission of guilt from the Army transcripts used to relieve me of my duties and discharge me without benefits.

Double jeopardy did not apply since my discharge was an administrative removal. This confused me. When I petitioned the commanding general for relief, it was explained to me that if I accepted, my discharge would be punitive.

I was incredibly confused and even more angry. I began to resent the very system I was willing to die for. Now, I could not even afford to defend myself. Once again, my class in society determined how much relief I could receive from society, and it is nonexistent when you are poor.

My wife and I pled guilty and received a fine, and we would be on federal probation until our fines were paid. We both now would carry felony convictions for the rest of our lives.

My probation officer was female. I was in the beginning of the throes of relapse. I tested positive for marijuana, and I was required to attend drug outpatient treatment with group therapy. Everyone in the group was on federal probation and on heavy narcotics.

This would lead to me meeting a new friend strung out on heroin. I began giving him a ride home after group therapy. When I discovered he was still using, the words of my grandfather began to haunt my thoughts: If you keep going to a barbershop, you eventually will get a haircut.

This proved true in my life as an addict that is angry at society. I eventually tried heroin, leading to my probation being revoked and a six-month prison sentence to be served at the Atlanta Federal Prison Camp, beginning on my birthday in 1999.

RLTW
November 27, 2022

## Atlanta Federal Prison Camp

I was given a reporting date to begin serving my sentence in July 1999. I would not report until November. I had separated from my wife. I was renting a room in a single wide trailer owned by my using buddy's sister.

I was splitting time between her house and the house where my wife and daughter were living. It was more convenient to stay with my daughter at the house she lives in, then trying to shuffle her around while I was using heroin.

I somehow decided to get a little help from methadone supplied by a clinic in Columbus. I shifted between that and heroin. I found methadone to be much more addictive than any other narcotic I ever consumed.

Replacing one substance with another in the life of an addict is counterintuitive to real recovery. It will provide a sense of normalcy if your goal is truly to get off narcotics. The hard truth is, the addict uses narcotics to mask whatever is going on inside their decision-making process.

The drug is the thing that covers the insecurities of addressing shortcomings. It is a small symptom of what drove a person to seek refuge in something we know will overcome us. I learned to compare it to a hamster in a cage with one of those round wheels.

The hamster can see what freedom looks like in his cage. The wheel is his coping mechanism. He gets on that wheel fully knowing it always ends up right back where the wheel started, getting nowhere fast. Yet still he gets on that wheel going nowhere. That is my stronghold.

I had known exactly where narcotics would take me since I was fifteen years old, and I first tried pills and powder substances, eventually bowing to the pressure of injecting heroin with guys I was working in construction with. I watched three friends overdose by the time I was seventeen.

I lost another few my first year in the Army. Somehow, I had managed to stay away from the allure of narcotics while serving. When I was accountable to only myself again, I fell back into the company of narcotics to suppress the mood swings I was having dealing with civilian hierarchies and societal rules.

I violated their rules by returning to addiction, and now I would have to pay the piper. But before I would report to prison, I would use heroin every day for fifty-seven days. I would get a ride from my wife and daughter to the federal prison camp. I crossed the Chattahoochee River twice on our way.

I began to ponder my time as a Ranger on Fort Benning. If I was ever going to return to sanity, I would have to look at exactly where it began to unravel in my life. Or did I ever have the sanity to unravel? No middle ground. When the wheels fall off John Burns's car, they all fall off!

I reported to the camp and was assigned to H dorm. My counselor kept his office in G dorm, so my stay in H dorm would be temporary. I did, however, meet the man who would ignite a desire to learn about the Jesus of the Bible in H dorm.

Willie Davis was a very large Black man. When he introduced himself to me, he could tell I was sick. I was going through withdrawals for a few days. He did, however, pose an interesting question: "White Boy, do you intend to leave here how you got here, or do you want to change yourself for the better?"

He handed me a Bible and invited me to an inmate church service on Wednesday evening. I was Catholic. I had not heard anyone address Jesus Christ this way since I first heard Dan Busch read me his Bible. Then I read in the Bible; from the mouth of two witnesses, God perfects praise.

I moved to G dormitory and made new friends. I was, for the first time in my life, experiencing time as a true minority. I was one of four White men in a dorm of a hundred people. We shared a common area, a common shower, and we had two men to each concrete cubicle.

I began to understand prison life and how it requires a hustle for survival. I won't give up my secrets, but I managed to come up with a few of my own that kept me in ice cream and honey buns, which I immediately gave to my cellmate, Lemuel George.

He and I spent many nights hashing out what was wrong with society. Why are narcotics in every minority neighborhood in

America? Does America incarcerate minorities as a means of keeping them from voting in elections? Is America inherently racist?

I have been White my entire life. I never contemplated any other struggle but my own. Now, I was in prison learning of struggles by people I did not look like. In the end, we are all just squirrels trying to store nuts for the winter!

I learned to accept people for who they are, not the labels society deems I adopt. I learned to take people one at a time. I held debates with men who told me they hated me, and in the end, we somehow managed to coexist in a very dangerous setting.

My time in the prison camp was marked by intense Bible study and writing speeches for a prison club I had joined called Speech Crafters. It gave me insight into the lives of men I never dreamed I would learn to call my prison family of brothers in Christ.

These men gave me another building block in my ever-increasing Christian foundation. They showed me practical Christian empathy as we all began to understand what drove us to incarceration together.

I finally began to understand how precious freedom is, only after mine had been taken away. No excuses. I believe God had allowed me to get to this point to remove presuppositions as to the limits of his love.

RLTW
November 27, 2022

## Nothing Makes Sense

I was released exactly six months to the day I reported to prison. While incarcerated, I learned a lot about the man I saw when I looked in the mirror. I had made a commitment to follow Dan Busch's example and never care what men think about me again. The only thing that matters is what God thinks.

I now had the Bible to lean on any time I encounter tribulation and temptation. I returned to Columbus, got a job building fences, and received my back pay for service-connected disability payments now that I left the prison. I eventually rented a house and joined a church.

As I enquired of the beliefs of the Assemblies of God, I decided I would discover their history before committing to any doctrines I may find as unscriptural. I enrolled my daughter in Christian pre-K and began a life as part of the church community.

I decided to study the history of the Bible and how we got the English King James translation. My journey took me through every empire in the book of Daniel, and I realized so many things the church was practicing that were not scriptural and bordering on polytheism.

I could not believe how the pastor justified prosperity when half of his congregation was in the military or retired and living just below the poverty line. I realized the only man to get paid for the gospel in the New Testament was Judas.

I searched for a new church home. They all were violating the first commandment. They had married the world system and were accepting tax breaks from the government for being designated as nonprofit. Jesus Christ said "Render unto Caesar that which is Caesar's."

Accepting tax breaks will lead to eventual persecution. The state controls what messages are now appropriate in Christian pulpits. There are now ministers serving in the Senate. Jesus Christ separated church and state when he washed his disciples' feet. True Christian leadership!

I began to rely wholly on the words of scripture, which ignited my desire to learn biblical Hebrew and Koine Greek. The Holy Spirit ignited a fire in my brain that has been in overdrive for twenty-two years and counting. I have become a Berean Christian out of Acts 17:11.

I began to reverse engineer the Bible by beginning my study of the book of Revelation. It caused me to study every other book of the Bible to understand its contents. Revelation was the only book of the Bible I read in prison that promised a blessing for reading it.

Now it was guiding every study I have ever done. I realized that most Christian denominations are anti-Semitic in their practice. They cling to New Testament–only theology, denying 87 percent of the rest of the Bible. Their religious traditions imported from Babylon have replaced sound Old Testament mercy.

Here is an abject lesson in double-minded thinking, JB-style.

I had been trained as a leader by the Seventy-Fifth Ranger Regiment. I never quit anything. Somehow, now I was rationalizing leaving the accountability of a church that was craving Christian leadership. I knew I should stay and continue studying and praying for what God wanted me to do. I got ahead of God.

Relapse was right around the corner. My frustration led me once again to link up with addict friends who were now smoking crack and shooting heroin. I was on supervised release. It was only a matter of time before I tested positive for dope. It came sooner than I expected.

My new probation officer required I go into an inpatient rehabilitation program. The next two years of my life would see me enter and complete six programs and relapse within moments of finishing. I also got kicked out of no-less-than three programs for using in the program.

I was now living in a van my buddy gave me. My wife and daughter had moved to Utah. My only structure of friends were all using dope of some form. I was working to support my addiction and, in some sick way, trying to get closer to God by studying the Bible every night in my van.

I was within a few months of completing probation. Anxiety had me get on methadone as I met the woman I would eventually marry and spend the last twenty-one years with. She was living in Atlanta, and as long as I stuck to methadone, I could travel to see her.

There are no words to describe my wife. She endured insanity in my life while I fought a war to get off illegal narcotics. I have had old injuries and even newer injuries that were serious enough to be prescribed narcotics.

I had to find the answer in the Bible.

For the weapons we fight with are spiritual, not carnal, for the pulling down of strongholds. In the Koine Greek tongue, strongholds are the word *pharmakia*. It is men who give us narcotics for the control of the mind. If America wanted to win the drug war, it could. Drugs make money.

Government exists to sow chaos. Politics require crisis. Politicians manufacture crisis in order to increase budgets, for the purpose of printing incredible amounts of money to deal with the crisis they manufactured. The money makes its way to the lobbyists in neighborhoods where it can be laundered.

Then taxes are raised to demand we foot the bill for the crisis they manufactured. Our grandchildren and six generations after them could work a hundred years each, and our national debt would not be paid. Our entire system requires a political elite class of people ordering our footsteps.

My faith is at odds with those who took the Bible and prayer out of public school. Now people who have never read the Bible are teaching our children God does not exist. My life has reached the point of no return. Christian insurrection is now my lot, and words are my tool.

RLTW
November 27, 2022

## A Ranger Wrestling Match

Returning to Columbus after my incarceration proved to be a great challenge. The seeds of Bible belief had been sown into my troubled mind. I had become obsessive-compulsive in the study of God's word.

I had joined the Assemblies of God. I had somehow managed to hold down a job in construction. I was separated from my wife, and I was sharing responsibility for raising my daughter. I was accountable to a probation officer alone. Little did I know, the shining one had set many traps.

With my history of abusing narcotics, I was required to complete an outpatient substance abuse program. I would once again be joining other addicts on supervised release, trying to adjust to a society that has labeled them as career felons.

The system required strict adherence to established social norms. The government is so entrenched in keeping up the narrative of fighting a drug war that addicts have become pawns in justifying increasing budgets and manpower to keep the prison industrial complex lucrative for politicians.

Law schools are full because our laws encourage lawless behavior. A class war is being waged by college-educated elitists who profit from the illicit narcotics industry. The government has no intention of winning the drug war in America. In fact, the war they are waging is not against suppliers; it is against users.

Government has always waged a war for the control of the flow of worldwide opium. History is littered with empires vying for control of the poppy plant and the drugs that are manufactured to supply the consumption mentality plaguing America like no empire in history.

Vietnam began with the narrative of stemming the Western expansion of communism. Once the CIA got involved, opium began to flow into America, and no inner-city neighborhood was spared. America had North Vietnam on the ropes until Richard Nixon announced his war on drugs.

Three trillion dollars has been spent fighting this war without end to date. Our cities are now being filled with a synthetic opioid manufactured by America's enemies. China and Mexico are entrenched in the manufacture and sale of illicit narcotics to American citizens. Our elected officials are implicit.

I have the unfortunate testimony of homeless in my repertoire. I had become disillusioned with the American dream. I believe our government exists to control every aspect of our lives. Narcotics are no different. The government is the largest drug dealer on our planet.

The pharmaceutical lobby is the largest lobby by far. They enjoy a relationship to our elected officials that is at least criminal. Their influence in writing laws that punish drug salesmen they do not control has become untenable. Delusion has manifested in America, and politicians cannot be trusted!

Whenever illicit narcotics became my crutch, government doctors at the Veterans Administration stepped in to prescribe their version of a legal narcotic. Control was ceded by myself, and I had let the wolves into my henhouse. My dealer now was Uncle Sugar!

Absolute power over my mind would need to be sacrificed to allow the government to solve the issue of addiction plaguing my life. Double-mindedness became my ally, and a long road awaited my footstep. I became voluntarily homeless and moved into my van under a bridge along the Chattahoochee River.

I began to hang out with numerous people hooked on crack cocaine. I myself dabbled in crack for a relatively short time. It did not do anything to help my obsessive-compulsive nature. I would be awake for days on end. Studying the Bible while homeless became my new drug.

Along the way, God began to show me our entire system, including the American church experience, which did not have God's pleasing, perfect will as their goal. Church and state exist to make money. God exists to forgive and show the love of Jesus Christ suspended between heaven and earth.

I began to see addicts as a product of the system that had no intention of helping them remain clean. There is way too much money entrenched in the federal and state budgets set aside to deal with addiction and incarceration. One interdependently supports the other.

American politicians and law enforcement officials need people addicted. Budgets are decided by projections about the number of people that will violate probation. Prisons are built, and the entire system feeds off the misery of poor folks who are addicted.

The prison industrial complex in America is real. The drug war has been manipulated by the people we elect, and they have no intention of fighting the real criminals flooding our rural neighborhoods with poisons that kill our unsuspecting children. Incarceration fuels greed in America.

Homeless people spend their lives most often running from a system that has failed them. The home is not what is missing from their lives. It is the love of the home that has disappeared from their lives.

Narcotics are where people who have lost their first love hibernate. The hamster-in-a-cage mentality takes over, and the system feeds their desire to segregate from the love of the home. Narcotics are where disenfranchised people begin to find refuge.

Look in the mirror to find out what is wrong with your addicted loved ones! They are missing the unconditional love the American dream once promised. Incarceration has become a tool of the government to increase budgets to deal with a crisis they are orchestrating.

Government will never wash anyone's feet! Jesus Christ does. He is the same yesterday, today, and tomorrow. He frees the imprisoned. He delivers those addicted to strongholds our government has no intention on eliminating.

Jesus Christ alone began to pull down the stronghold of addiction plaguing my existence. I had to see this world through his eyes, and his eyes wrote the entire Bible before he spoke our universe into existence.

*He was crucified upon a cross of wood, yet he*
*created the hill upon which it stood.*
*He is alive forevermore, and he is returning*
*for his virgin bride very soon.*

RLTW
December 12, 2022

# GRACE

# GEORGIA ON MY MIND

I managed to finish my supervised release. My fines were all paid. I could once again make my own choices. I decided to move to Atlanta and enter the VA methadone program. The year was 2002.

America had been attacked while I was in the throes of addiction. I had been introduced to Islam in Somalia. I had learned the very American and militant brand of Islam taught to inmates in federal prison. These men are angry, and Louis Farrakhan fuels that anger.

The Nation of Islam is inherently racist. I do, however, understand their frustration. I wish they would understand why they still struggle. The politicians that pretend to represent Black communities have left their inner city and poor rural communities destitute for fatherhood.

I listened intently to men who boiled with hatred of me for being White. As I listened, I began to realize I needed to find out why. The two-party system had failed these incarcerated men for four generations. Their mothers were now raising their great-grand-children as Black men serving long prison sentences.

While incarcerated, I learned the history through my own eyes. The very political party that has always been on the wrong side of racial division had come up with a plan to destroy the moral fabric in the Black community.

These eugenic-minded politicians have enriched themselves by incarcerating Black men. Joe Biden authored the 1994 crime bill as the Democrat answer for crime occurring in Black neighborhoods. They once again created a false narrative to engineer a crisis.

Money was printed and laundered in these poor communities. Drugs flowed as politicians did absolutely nothing to confront the inherently racist policy. Selling powder cocaine occurs mostly in White circles. Freebase cocaine had ravaged the Black community disproportionally.

I wondered if invading Panama in 1989 fueled the need for Mexican cartels to get into the business of cocaine. America has spent three trillion dollars in the drug war since 1968. They cannot keep a joint elementary school. It leads me to believe they are complicit with the cartels.

Two industries make money for politicians in both political parties: the drug industry, both legal and illegal; and the prison industry, which competes with the military industrial complex for exclusivity in political circles. United Prison Corporation is the prison system controlled by the Congress. It is criminal!

The 1994 crime bill targeted the sale of crack cocaine when it began to affect White people in suburban communities. Only then did the Congress act. Joe Biden targeted young Black men as he came up with mandatory minimum sentences for the sale of crack cocaine.

The term *kingpin* became vernacular as the Senate moved to designate Black gangs as continuous criminal enterprises carrying a mandatory life sentence. This was all orchestrated by Democrats in the Senate and signed into law in 1994 by William Jefferson Clinton.

Now I found myself incarcerated with Black men I came to admire even if I did not agree with them. I understood the allure of Islam when you are angry at the system that has failed your family for generations.

I began to adopt the policy of hard truths over easy lies governing what the spirit inside me was saying. I began to confront my own inherent racism: being raised in an all-White neighborhood and all-White church, playing pretend while fearing Black people. Stereotypes over substance.

I began to see that the government never touches anything that turns to gold. Policies promising to lift people out of poverty have only created more poverty.

The removal of the Black man from the community, coupled with the destruction of manufacturing, has crippled most Black women and harnessed them to government-sponsored programs.

Take away income earners and take away jobs, you can harness people to failure for years as you give them handouts while enriching yourself. A caste system hiding in plain sight. A new type of slave master disguised as a savior. Who is advocating for these communities?

When America lost the prophet sent from God to educate us of his own internal struggle, radicals adopted a plan. This was counterintuitive to achieving his vision of a new America. Content of character was replaced with advocating first for the color of one's skin.

Dr. King believed in the entire Bible. He understood God's plans for the fledgling nation of Israel emerging after the holocaust. He quoted Moses as he prophesied of his own demise.

The mountaintop would not be achieved in his lifetime, and he was okay with loving Jesus Christ while in the greatest valley of his own life. His vision was one of unity. Does that match the replacement theology that grew out of the Black liberation theology adopted after Dr. King's death?

Dr. King believed Jesus Christ died for all sinners. Now the Bible and prayer had been removed from the lives of Black children in public education. The Bible tenets that had driven Dr. King's dream were abandoned for new religious traditions adopted in homes where the Bible was read by all previously.

Public schools began experiencing government legislated desegregation, while that same government judiciously removed the Bible and prayer from the children's learning experience. Kids began to realize their ancestors were inherently eugenic, most often leading to closet-practiced racism in segregated communities.

The government was advocating for teaching children to be racist based on the color of one's skin. One book answers the question of race better than any, and now the government has succeeded in legislating that book out of your child's life.

Teachers became implicit in racist ideology being purported by those who control the flow of information to our children. Public school became the social engineering project the radicals in power engineered to keep common people in a state of chaos.

America needs a new prophet with God's vision for utopia, front and center, if we are to ever solve the problem of government-engineered racial division. God will have to raise up prophets again.

His name is Yeshua Hamashiach, Jesus the Christ to us born-again believers.

## Where Are We in Time

Charles Dickens begins *A Tale of Two Cities* with the statement "It was the best of times, and it was the worst of times."

Are we witnessing the same conundrums in our world today? Is the religion of ancient Babylon uniting before our eyes as the whole world seems to be united in stopping God's plan for Jerusalem?

Politics is the art of deception. Adam and Eve were the first voters in history. Their choice revolved around believing the word of the God who created them for the purpose of fellowship or allowing a politician dressed as a serpent to get us to question God's written word.

The two-party system in America has deceived true believers in God. One party openly advocates for the destruction of all things Christians and Jews believe. One side mixes a little bit of outward piety, with an unwavering devotion to the cult of Mithras, masquerading as the bull of Wall Street.

Neither side has God's ideas about civilization in mind. God's ideas about absolute morality hinges upon the knowledge of his preconceived plan for those created in his image. Humans were placed in the garden as a part of God's plan to redeem his creation from the original usurper.

Today, elements in both parties openly mock God in their devotion to a cause that is steeped in delusion. We poor believers in a cause greater than ourselves are now under attack for having faith in God's single plan of redemption as outlined in the greatest piece of literature ever conceived.

After forty-five years of reading the Bible consistently and studying it for thirty-two years now and counting, I can say without a doubt that according to what science knows about our present reality, I am convinced that the Bible is the only book conceived entirely outside of how humans experience time.

I had to lose every religious presupposition and focus on the Bible as literature. I never experienced a piece of literature that seemed to have more than one prose occurring at one time while all pointing to one event in all human history. I was reading a book that was most misunderstood.

I had learned a few codes while serving our country. I had learned about rules in code writing. The goal is to get a message to someone while hiding it from those who will use it for their own purposes. The way the code writer achieves this is to spread the true message out within the entire body of the letter.

In this case, God the creator has spread his entire message out over sixty-six books, revealed to over forty men, within a 3,000-year time period, explaining every day of human history in advance. The creator of the universe has left us an owner's manual over his entire creation, with a warranty deed of the cross!

From the first sentence in Genesis, till the final chapter in Revelation, the message is consistent. God is the creator who intended to save humanity by becoming the Son of God in the womb of a virgin Jewish girl, the only baby ever born knowing the exact hour and minute he would die.

His death would lead to his promised inheritance. The resurrection guaranteed that God's plan to place Jesus Christ on David's throne in Jerusalem was now moving toward the climax of human history. Before Christ receives his kingdom, he must first receive his virgin bride.

The bride would be taken from all the nations of the earth, from all the Gentile tribes of the earth, while national Israel was temporarily separated from their land. This separation of time was prophesied by Christ as beginning in Ephesus and ending sometime during the Laodicean church age.

This church age has lasted 1,983 years and counting. God has begun regathering national Israel in the land he gave Abraham. We are living in the times the prophet Asaph warned us would befall Israel in the last days. The Jews are back in the land and prospering.

Messianic congregations are sprouting in Israel and Jerusalem—the Orthodox priests who yearn for a return to the law of Moses, when they held all the power, and who, right now, are calling for the expulsion of ministries from evangelical Christianity.

We have returned to the time of the Acts of the Apostles. America is in the final stage of the abandonment wrath of God manifesting. We have been warned for twenty-one years and counting to return God to the center of our lives again. Yet mankind has doubled down in the mocking of God.

Sexual perversion and the all-out assault on the marriage covenant reveal that God must return to judging America, or he will have to resurrect and apologize to Sodom and Gomorrah. Look for the return of fallen angels to enter sexual intercourse once again with the daughters of men.

These are all events prophesied in the Bible. Men have become lovers of themselves. No one cares for the creator who gave us everything. He must bring judgment upon a world that has denied His very existence. Pride always comes before a great fall. Apathy in America had led us here.

No one serves causes greater than themselves anymore. It is all about "What is in it for me?" I never thought I would live to see America use all its freedom to separate from the God who shed his grace on thee. And it only took two generations!

The Bible identifies where we are right now in history. The only way to know is to return to a personal relationship to the Messiah through his entire written revealed word, written by him and the Trinity before they spoke our universe into existence.

The Bible is the guide to understanding the entire mind of God and his single plan of redemption. It is the most preposterous debt payment plan in history. It revolves around a loving God who gave his willing Son, on a lonely hill, where they nailed him to his divine destiny for my sins!

RLTW
May 27, 2023

# The Warrior Conundrum

My life in Atlanta shifted to learning to deal with the aftermath of combat trauma. I was enrolled in outpatient PTSD counseling, and I began to incorporate my faith into learning exactly how peace is nothing more than a stubbornly persistent illusion to those who have prosecuted war.

Doctors were more than willing to offer an opinion based upon what they learned in medical school. I was confused for I was reading the Bible, which contains stories of great men and women who waged war.

The Bible identified differences between righteous killing and murder. King David became my example for learning to experience some semblance of peace. It would never look like man's manufactured ideas about peace, for all the thoughts of man are only evil continually. Men wage war for monetary purposes.

I believed all wars are man's inventions. God will give you the desires of your heart to prove that he alone is God. Men wage war for human reasons about what "civilized" looks like. Hiding in plain sight is the Greek term *eugenics*. Nations believe they are exceptional without God.

America was indeed attacked on September 11, 2001. However, the gradual fall away from biblical beginnings led to the rise in Islamic radicalism, as America looked to secure the petrodollar while allowing for all the immoral policies our government backed to be emigrated abroad.

Anyone who has ever traveled east of Jerusalem can tell you that religion is what guides every decision made by rulers. Islam cannot exist within the confines of representative government of any kind. It is itself a theocracy, backed and advanced by militant government. It is about conquest!

Roman Catholicism is about the marriage of government to state. While pretending to practice outward piety, the church of Rome is hording enough wealth to solve world hunger! Both Islam and Catholicism emigrated from Babylon. Both will play an important role in the rise of the satanic trinity.

I continued in my Catholic faith while being deployed to combat. I figured it could not hurt having a priest absolve me of my sin. If I was to die, purgatory awaited, and I could negotiate with God after dying for my country. I later learned this is the great lie of Catholicism and the reason they do not want their followers learning the Bible.

Warfare has taught me how arrogant men in power have become. Ever willing to send a poor class of citizen to battlefields most Americans know not exist, all for the purpose of keeping them wealthy and in complete power. The sacrifice of American children matters not to them as long as their kids do not have to fight.

While in treatment at the VA, I continued to confront racism in my own life. I had befriended many Black veterans who I listened to, as they described segregation, service, and life after Vietnam and Korea. I realized that our country has been built upon a bad foundation.

The word in English is *eugenics*. It was coined by the Greeks to describe a well-born stock of people who should benefit from education, commerce, and religion. Their desire is to enslave an undereducated population to labor as they are the sole benefactors of wealth.

Nowhere on earth has eugenics taken root like it has in America. I began to realize our education system actually promotes a version of eugenics that may prove to be the most diabolical form of racism and classism ever advanced by humans.

The cult of Charles Darwin hides in plain sight as highly educated elite people harness the rest of society to their version of utopia, completely devoid of the knowledge of God or his Bible. By removing the Bible and prayer from public school, rich elitists could keep poor folks in slavery, and the government agreed.

Charles Darwin was born into a wealthy ruling family in England. He was an advocate for White eugenics. He thought Black people were the result of not fully evolving from monkeys. He did not believe in intelligent design because he believed only one class of people could possibly be intelligent.

His theory on the origin of the species permeates and harnesses our entire education system to inherent classism and racism. Our American society is breaking down morally because they undermined our biblical heritage and advanced a eugenic model on our society.

Sadly, this model made it into Western seminary. The history of racism in church cannot be overstated. The KKK came from the Southern Baptist convention. Black liberation theology was birthed upon the death of Martin Luther King Jr. Church has caused more division than unity.

Replacement theology was adopted by the church in Ephesus and addressed by Jesus Christ in his letter to the Ephesian church. Western seminary practices Greek hermeneutics, which is not scriptural. The writers of the Bible practiced Hebrew hermeneutics.

The Old Testament was revealed to men in Hebrew. It was transliterated into Greek by Pharaoh Ptolemy in 265 BC. The language of conquest replaced God's single creation: love language. From this transliteration, every empire in history translated the Bible into a new conquest language.

Inadvertently, men have succumbed to being dumbed down in church as they adopted a New Testament–only theosophy, and there is no longer Holy Spirit–power emanating from church pulpits.

As a soldier home while my peers were fighting a protracted war on terrorism, I decided I needed to get right with the God of the Bible and learn the ancient Hebrew language and Greek New Testament. I soon realized that the Bible was one complete message, divided into two Testaments by men!

War began to take the lives of men I respected and who loved Jesus Christ. The only way I can honor them is to speak hard truths and leave easy lies in the vestibule of the church. The Bible is now my warranty deed and owner's manual for all things pertaining to God, for men are most double-minded.

My journey gets lonely, but I would rather be alone with God than surrounded by people who care nothing about the creator who purchased their eternal life on Calvary. My destiny has been chosen by God, my redeemer, and I know my redeemer lives!

RLTW
March 26, 2023

# Understanding Biblical Strongholds

My love for the Bible shifted into overdrive after moving to Atlanta and experiencing what most humans would call a sense of normalcy. I was attending church services, reading my Bible, and settling in to my relationship with my new bride.

We had rented a house close to the Veterans Administration hospital, where I was attending drug outpatient therapy. I was taking methadone daily, all the while asking myself a rational question: Have I replaced one horrible addiction with another sanctioned by medical professionals? What does God think?

I had begun to understand that we are indeed pawns in a spiritual battle between God and Lucifer. I had made the decision to accept Christ's debt payment plan. I believed the blood of God's lamb had covered my unrighteousness, yet I was still caught up in addiction to methadone.

I understood that we are justified by faith. What I did not realize is that this is where our journey in Christ begins. It is not over when we accept the most preposterous debt payment plan in human history. When a human accepts Christ's testimony of himself, Lucifer musters his fallen-angel army to stop you from fulfilling God's perfect, pleasing will.

For the weapons we fight with are spiritual, not carnal, for the pulling down of strongholds. We are indeed in a battle. Christ is our divine protector, and he is the one who fights for us. His only requirement is for Christians to become noble Bereans and search the scripture daily.

Revelation reveals that those Christ loves, he chastens. No one enjoys being told they are wrong, especially after they have accepted Christ's mercy. Salvation begins and ends with the eternal mercy from God. Mercy is all about biblical correction and the humility to admit each day that we are sinners.

The year 2003 saw my faith shift to understanding the entire Bible from a literature perspective. I figured the Bible was a book I needed to know how it was conceived and by whom. Religion taught me God revealed it to men over time.

I believed the word was conceived by Elohim the creator before he spoke the universe into existence. Now, I was beginning to see history in the pages of the Bible. An obsessive-compulsive nature had been my conundrum since birth, and I decided to apply that to Bible study.

I had read that all scripture was God-breathed. That meant the Old Testament is as important as the New Testament. My knowledge of construction led me to believe that God would never build his house upon a foundation that was not ancient. What I learned astounded me.

I began to realize that the entire New Testament was concealed in the Old Testament. I realized the entire Old Testament was revealed in the person of Jesus Christ in the New Testament.

What really excited me was the knowledge that Jesus Christ was indeed the writer of the entire Bible in eternity past. Not only was he the writer, but every letter and number pointed to his first and second advents.

I had read that all scripture was available for reproof and correction. No other book claims to correct itself by only looking to other books of the Bible for the correction or understanding needed. This is how I began to discern that most Western preachers rely on other men's writings about the Bible.

Western seminary denies 87 percent of scripture each time they claim the Gentiles replaced national Israel in God's single plan of redemption. I learned that church in America long ago left solid Old Testament foundations to convince other men that they alone hold the keys to understanding God.

I realized a hostage crisis was taking place in church on Wednesday and Sunday. It was simple for me. God is not the respecter of persons. He wrote the Bible and gave us the chance to receive the Holy Spirit for the distinct purpose of teaching us his truth. No need for preachers.

In my own life, this was playing out with my addiction to methadone. Preachers who I trusted were condemning me. I tried to find one place in the Bible where Christ condemned. It has been twenty-plus years, and I still only find mercy in Christ ministry.

The Old Testament laid the groundwork for Gentiles to become fellow heirs with the remnant of Jewish believers in Messiah that God has always maintained. God's propensity to show mercy is not something he does; it is actually who he is! Mercy is his divine attribute all believers should strive to understand.

All scripture is prophetic. The plan of God was carried out by the players in the Old and New Testaments, exactly how God wrote the script. The sooner you settle in your heart that you are a pawn in a divine love drama written by the God of creation in eternity past, the sooner the Bible can be rightly divided.

These revelations began to come to me in the throes of addiction, which led to me beginning to understand that God is indeed in control. Sovereignty is often misunderstood as humans look to blame sin on free will. Sin is how I began to realize God intended to save me in spite of sin.

Forgiveness is what was needed in my life. I had to allow God to forgive me, then I could begin to overcome the stronghold that plagued my human existence.

Mercy led me to study the ancient Greek manuscript where the word *stronghold* became real to me.

The word *stronghold* in Koine Greek written by Paul is the word *pharmakia*. It is taken from the root word *pharma*. In God's eyes, strongholds are a product of pharmaceuticals. Narcotics are one more way Satan tries to stop the plans of God for your life from coming to pass.

He was wounded for our transgressions, he was bruised for our iniquities, the chastisement of us is upon him, and by his stripes, we are healed. Choose this day to accept healing of the flesh from Christ and claim the promise of Isaiah 53 to overcome addiction.

RLTW
March 26, 2023

## God's Time

God begins the Bible narrative with an allusion to time. The phrase "In the beginning" has caused great division in our world. At war is God's reality versus man's perception of reality. God's reality we call faith. Men's perception of reality we call religion.

The creator of the universe we call home told our story before it unfolded. The sovereignty of God is outlined in the pages of the Bible. From Genesis to Revelation, God went out of his way to explain to humans that they are pawns in a predetermined love drama.

God exists completely outside of how humans experience time. Our time is outlined in scripture. God is eternal. He is the definition of infinity. If science wants to solve the infinity question, they should return to the math and science of creation outlined in scripture.

The word *beginning* is a statement God made to relate when he began the process of creating our world inhabitable for men. The Bible states that our world was created perfect. Yet Genesis 2 claims that the world became without form and void.

The word *became* requires a change: going from one form to another. This seems to insinuate that something caused our creator to allow the earth to become without form and void. The Bible teaches that God began to move the world then, from chaos to order.

The narrative begins on day 1. Science aligns with the six-day narrative, all the while trying to refute an intelligent designer over creation.

The laws of entropy were established by God in Genesis 1. God began restoring order by moving away from the chaos caused by Lucifer's rebellion, sometime between the beginning and day 1 of creation. Entropy is the movement from chaos to order.

Our story does not begin with Adam. It begins with the knowledge of the order of creation. God created four things: the heavens, of which there are three outlined in scripture; the earth; angels, to include the cherubim, the seraphim, and the archangels.

There are three archangels: Lucifer, the anointed cherub that covereth, of the Ezekiel 28 and Isaiah 14 narrative; Michael, the guardian and warrior angel protecting the offspring of Abraham, and Gabriel, the angelic messenger.

There are no female angels.

This is very important to begin to understand why God created man in his own image. Only humans were created for the distinct purpose of being saved. The unique role a woman plays in salvation should put to bed how God sees equality between the genders.

A woman possesses the most exalted tabernacle in human history. Her womb is where the matrix of Numbers 12 begins its journey. The Matrix is the thirty-three trillion cells that make up the tabernacle of the human condition. We are a spirit that possesses a soul while occupying a tabernacle we call the body.

Humans are a product of a war going on between Lucifer, and the one-third of the angels who followed him in his rebellion, and the God of creation. Humans were uniquely created to replace the heavenly angelic worshippers who followed Lucifer in his rebellion. True replacement theology!

Albert Einstein is given credit for his quantum theory, identifying time as a companion to the three spatial dimensions of length, width, and height. Paul gave us his quantum theory in Ephesians 3:18 that holds the key to distinguishing what is most important to God.

Time is most important to God. It is more important than the three-dimensional space you occupy on Sunday or Wednesday. Jesus Christ requires a believer to spend time in scripture every day, if they intend to be counted noble enough to rule and reign with him in his coming kingdom.

Jesus's time is found in his own admission: "I am the light of the world." Christ was saying that "I am the creator who spoke light into existence on day 1. I clothed man in my light. Darkness caused man to question my word and touch and eat of the tree of the knowledge of good and evil." Its time had not come yet to be partaken of, for that tree would become the cross of Christ in AD 32 on Passover.

God is sovereign over the affairs of men. He determines life and death. Eternal life is to be clothed in the light of Christ, a return to being the new-creation relationship enjoyed by Adam and Eve, until the serpent beguiled them. To be born again is to be clothed in light from the Messiah.

The light of day 1 was different from the light of the sun and moon established on day 4. Interestingly, modern science still wrestles with the speed of light. The methods of measuring light have accelerated in this century with the discoveries in physics.

If scientists would accept the Bible narrative and learn the ancient Hebrew language as it pertains to numerical valuations assigned to letters, I believe discovery will again point to God as sole creator. He is the light of the world who laid down his life for a world that deserves not his forgiveness.

God keeps Bible time much differently than men keep time. Learn Bible time, and you will indeed become a light in this world. God gave us human time in advance.

Our entire history was revealed in advance when God gave Moses the Torah on Sinai and continued all the way through the Apostolic period ending with Jesus Christ's Revelation, as given to John.

The Bible is a miraculous book of divine literature: sixty-six individual books, ascribed to at least forty authors, revealed over 3,000 years, all pointing to Christ dying, Christ being buried, and Christ rising again.

The most preposterous debt payment plan in human history, all conceived by the Trinity of creation, and revealed to men in God time, as he unlocked the mystery of our past, our present, and our future as believers or nonbelievers. Freedom to choose as a gift from God!

RLTW
March 27, 2023

## Babylonian Time vs. Jerusalem Time

Is the Garden of Eden the city of Jerusalem? The garden had many varieties of trees. Yet only one tree held the knowledge of good and evil. Was the reason Adam and Eve were told that they could not touch or eat of this tree a time equation?

Leviticus 25 teaches us about when to plant a sapling, how often the sapling needs pruning, when not to eat the fruit, and when exactly to harvest the fruit of the tree. We are taught that fruit is to be harvested and shared in the fourth season. What millennium held the key to Christ's Crucifixion?

Does the Bible identify how old Jesus Christ was during the Crucifixion? Jesus Christ is the seed, the vine, the branch, and was crucified upon the tree of the knowledge of good and evil. Why? Because Jesus Christ is the only man ever born for the purpose of dying upon a tree.

And God said "Let light be!" If there was ever an argument for light being instantaneous, this should qualify. God established light as being the source of life. Find the origin of light, and life becomes real.

The mathematics of creation points to light being instantaneous and, in a vacuum, existing outside of how human time is reckoned. Humans measure time through artificial means. They time how long light waves take to bend around objects. Can God time be measured?

Day 1 ended with the framing of how God rightly views human time. The evening and the morning were the first day. The Hebrew states *the erev* and *the boker*.

*Erev* is evening. It is when darkness makes all things appear indiscernible. Morning is *boker*. This is an allusion to light appearing. In God's economy, light always replaces darkness! The Bible day begins at sunset/moonrise. It lasts twenty-four hours until the next moonrise.

This is a very important biblical principle to begin understanding that every day in human history appears to occur in the Bible chronology. The entire Bible is written upon the Babylonian lunisolar calendar of thirty-day months, from moon cycle to moon cycle.

The Babylonians under Nimrod gave us the pagan calendar of twelve months based on the twelve constellations found common to all who view them. The Babylon calendar begins in January, ending in December. The Bible calendar is an agricultural calendar based upon three trees: the fig tree, the almond tree, and the olive. All three of these fruits can be harvested twice in a single season. The Bible outlines national Israel and the body of Christ as allegories. Only a few are chosen during the first harvest. Most go through a severe chastening before being harvested by Christ.

The Hebrew religious calendar begins with the birth of new lambs each spring in the month of Nisan. Lambs bound for the temple sacrifice have always been born in spring and only in the town of Bethlehem, even to this day while occupied by Edomites!

Jesus Christ as the lamb of God, I believe was born on Nisan 1. He was circumcised on day 8, inspected by the people of Jerusalem and priests of the temple on Nisan 10, then crucified on Nisan 14. He walked out of the garden tomb on Nisan 17. The pattern was established on Noah's ark!

Six days the Trinity set about creating our world inhabitable for us. He rested on the seventh day. Have you ever thought about what was missing on day 7? How about the evening and the morning? Why? The Sabbath rest is about an idle mind focusing on God for twenty-four hours. No human calendar!

Is it a coincidence the world east of Jerusalem is on a 360-day lunisolar calendar and the world west of Jerusalem is on a solar 365-day calendar? Is it a coincidence that every language east of Jerusalem is written from right to left, while every language west of Jerusalem is written from left to right?

Prophecy in the Bible is about prologue and pattern. God wrote the Bible and the entire timeline of human history in advance. A return to the Bible calendar in dealing with all things God makes the Bible easy to discern for all those Christ has called.

Western religion has married the world with its Babylonian pantheon. Believing grace is about God overlooking paganism in church is both naive and wanting! Will God forgive preachers for leading their flocks in the mixing of a little bit of baby Jesus with a whole lot of Nimrod?

I always fancied myself as someone who believed the world was too organized for our existence to be a random accident. The narrative of public education coupled with religion had led me further from the true knowledge of God. A change had to occur in my thinking.

While living a mile from the Chattahoochee River in Atlanta, I began to contemplate what parts of my testimony God could use and how he wanted me to proceed with my faith. Bible study became my escape, as I began to separate from all the things church was advancing that were not scriptural.

God had begun to reveal his will to me through scripture study while I was in the valley of addiction. I decided to throw in the towel. From this moment forward in 2003, my life would be subject to biblical correction from Jesus Christ.

Being born again became real, as I realized the more I focused on Jesus Christ in scripture, the more God began to lift the veil of addiction from my eyes. As the biblical knowledge of God's Messiah increased in my life, the less drugs helped! I was indeed understanding the new birth.

I now had to become Christlike and begin to offer mercy with all those I encountered. Mercy is my cry over my own life each day as I humbly appeal to God to order my footsteps into eternity.

2023

## Religion vs. Faith

I had to understand the difference. I set out years ago to discern why every religion I ever experienced shared the same hallmarks. Faith to me was my individual system of belief in an intelligent designer I refer to as God. Why does everybody have their own ideas about God?

Pride is the number 1 problem facing humans. The prouder you become of your own ability, the more you will worship all things men crave. Church in America is no different. I turn only to the evidence of denominationalism. At its core, it divides, even believers.

I spent a great part of my life training and serving in war zones. I had traveled to forty-five countries on five continents by the time I had turned twenty-seven. I had experienced all claims men make to having a monopoly on the idea of God. How could I decide which one was right?

It seems religion requires a three-dimensional space from where the idea of God can be packaged, sold, and corroborated with enough participants. Religion pointed to the worship of created things and created deities. Mythology is the backbone of all human religion.

The Babylonian mythology permeates the lives of Americans who claim faith in Jesus Christ. All denominations mix a little bit of baby Jesus with a whole lot of outward piety, and then combine this with the Babylonian pantheon to include marriage to the state calendar.

The Babylonian pantheon combined solar or sun worship with moon worship, and the first hint of astrology as Semiramis, the consort of Nimrod polluted the Mazzaroth of Job 38. This is the twelve constellations able to be viewed by all humans each evening.

The Mazzaroth, when viewed in their order of brightness, teaches the story of God's promised plan of redemption. The Mazzaroth begins with a virgin who gives birth to a lamb who becomes the lion of the tribe of Judah. All ancient religions seem to have learned the Mazzaroth from the fallen angels.

The servants of Nebo rounded out the Babylonian pantheon. These were the rich, elite nobles who were temple priests serving the high priest Nimrod in Babel. The high priest assumed the title Pontifex Maximus, which is the primary title of the Pope in Rome. Julius Caesar assumed this title.

In Persia, religion revolved around the house of the moon god and the ancient religion of astronomy practiced by the magi. This was a hereditary priesthood, the modern iteration we refer to as Islam.

Alexander the Great melded these three ancient religions with the sun worship going on in Egypt. He melded the Greek pantheon with Medo-Persia and Egypt to set up his capitol in Babylon on the Euphrates. He modeled his government after Cyrus the Great.

Sociopolitical elite men controlled the religions of Egypt, Assyria, Babylon, Medo-Persia, Greece, and Rome and set an example being followed to the last letter here in America. Mystery Babylon in my opinion is the system set up by Nimrod that permeates our new world order.

The American system of government mirrors the government of Nimrod. We have given it modern labels. However, hard truths reveal that religion indeed is an arm of government. Faith in God's plan requires I worship him alone as creator.

Religion requires a mediator between God and men. Denominational Christianity is no different. In fact, Jesus Christ says the reformation church of Sardis is a dead church in need of true resurrection. The marriage to the world by the church under Constantine continues today hiding in plain sight.

I struggled with religion my entire life. I question everything and accept nothing without evidence. I had read the Bible since I was ten. I had traveled east of Jerusalem to experience the world's religions. It seemed they all compromise with true belief in God as creator.

I have met and conversed with Muslims, Hindus, Catholics, Jews, denominational Christians, Jehovah's Witnesses, agnostics, and atheists. They all invited me to their own ideas about the house of God.

I figured if God existed, I wanted him to be able to solve my issues, and I wanted him to be too big to kidnap in any human structure built. If God existed, he was the creator holding everything I was witnessing together, even when war looked like it was all falling apart.

Religion pointed always to what I was doing: sinning, not going to church, not keeping Sabbath, not fasting enough, and not giving enough to the poor. Religion made me incredibly tired. I figured God wanted to give me rest from my human shortcomings. If heaven existed, it had to be better than here!

The Bible alone allowed me to see everything I had ever experienced. The characters of the Bible were exactly like me: flawed individuals with the humility to know they needed help from the creator. The Bible alone outlines the human condition. All have sinned and fall short of the glory of God.

Religion always points to division, segregating based upon your own understanding of God. Religion causes more people to deny the existence of an intelligent designer than it does convince. Religion is indeed the invention of man as taught by the cult of fallen-angel worshippers begun in Babylon.

Religion, when left unchecked, will always devolve into legalism. Only faith in God the creator of the Bible requires an acknowledgement of sin ensnaring us. Sin can all be summed up in exchanging the worship of the creator by replacing him with the worship of all things created. True human religion!

Men indeed claim a belief in God. God alone says, "I am the creator. Worship only me! I have given you a timeline of human history called the Bible." Study to show yourself approved, and human religion will melt away in favor of true faith in God alone working out your salvation.

Faith is all about what Jesus Christ is doing! It begins by believing in what he has done for us. He died so we might live. The greatest exchange program in human history. My guilt exchanged for Christ's innocence. All summed up in the mercy and grace of God!

RLTW
March 27, 2023

## The Jordan River

The river at the center of Jesus Christ's ministry is most misunderstood. I believe it happens to be one of the four rivers proceeding from Eden. Jordan is synonymous with "crossing over." To cross Jordan, old things fade away, and all things must become new.

Christians understand Jordan from the perspective of the baptism of Jesus Christ by John. Without tracing the history of why John came baptizing for the remission of Israel's sins, another doctrine of men has been adopted, adding works to grace.

The descendants of Jacob had gone down into Egypt as a family. Joseph, the chosen son, had been sold into slavery by his brothers.

He became the prime minister of Egypt. The sovereignty of God was on display as he alone protected Joseph in order to fulfill his word.

The deception by Abram over Pharaoh when he told him Sarai was his sister now plagued Jacob, as his offspring reproduced in Egypt and became more powerful than the Egyptian population. Steven in Acts 7 supplies the identity of the Pharaoh who knew not Joseph. He was an Assyrian.

This Assyrian Pharaoh enslaved the Hebrews for four hundred years and built many of the monuments in Luxor. God, however, decided it was time to raise up a deliverer. He prepares the daughter of Pharaoh to become Moses's mother and teacher in Egypt.

The Hebrews apparently had gotten comfortable in Egyptian slavery. It was two Hebrew witnesses who scared Moses into the desert of Midian, as he feared they would alert Pharaoh to the knowledge that he killed the Egyptian taskmaster. This, too, was part of God's plan to prepare the deliverer.

Moses would spend forty years in the desert of Midian, perhaps preparing him for the forty-year desert wondering where he would lead Israel into. He had to learn to become a shepherd and priest. Jethro provided his theology instruction, while Moses tended the sheep for his fledgling family.

Moses receives a bride in Midian. Learning patience in relationship would help Moses later as he dealt with the stiff-necked Israelites who had gotten completely comfortable in pagan Egypt as slaves. Moses would view Jordan from the heights above the Midian desert for forty years.

The desert of Midian is where God prepared Moses to receive the Torah. Deserts are synonymous with the lack of living water. What was missing in the lives of the Hebrews was the word of God. Egyptian law forbade the Hebrews from sacrificing to YHWH. Only Egypt's gods could be worshipped.

Moses was the brother to Pharaoh's firstborn son. He had been raised as an Egyptian. He was a direct threat to Pharaoh, and Moses feared this. I believe this may be what caused his stutter. The knowledge that killing the Egyptian by an heir to the throne of Egypt was treasonous.

Nonetheless, God's power was on display as he dealt with the Egyptian pantheon of gods through ten specific plagues, culminating in the death of the firstborn. Moses was now the only heir to the throne of Egypt unless Pharaoh released the Hebrews.

The last plague convinced Pharaoh that Moses's God is the God who controls every aspect of his creation. Pharaoh instructs the Egyptians to load Israel down with the treasures of Egypt to bring into their land and sanctify to their God. This act by Pharaoh would haunt Israel.

The treasures of Egypt and the fear of the unknown would cause the fledgling nation called out of pagan bondage to request a return to their previous existence. This occurred after God destroyed the entire Egyptian army in the Red Sea.

This sea was where the Nile River flowed. God showed them who controls rivers! All the gods of Egypt revolved around the control of the rains in Ethiopia, which is at the center of the entire Egyptian religion. Now Israel entered the desert where Moses spent forty years. They were all full of fear.

Disobedience leads to the golden calf incident in the valley below Sinai. While Moses was receiving the Ten Commandments, the Hebrews were already looking and acting like the world they had been called out of.

God decides he will allow Israel to wonder in the Midian desert for forty years. I have friends that have walked from Egypt to Jerusalem through Jordan, and they say it took them eleven days. Why forty years?

God reveals that no Israelite who complained about manna in the desert over forty years would live to enter the promised land. They would all perish for complaining, as God separated a remnant that would be faithful to him after entering the promised land. Moses would not live to cross the Jordan with the fledgling nation.

Moses returns to Israel during the seventieth week of Daniel as one of the two witnesses of Revelation. Moses gets it right the second time, as he is once again rejected by secular Israel, yet his testimony during the time of Jacob's trouble leads to national revival in Israel during the last half of the tribulation.

Before Israel could cross the Jordan and receive her tribal inheritance in the promised land, God had to separate the wheat from the chaff. All those who desired a return to Egyptian bondage and pagan religion would have to be purged.

Only those God could use in his proposed kingdom could cross Jordan. Our reward as the virgin bride of Christ is no different. If God cannot use you in the coming kingdom of his son, you, too, will have to be purged during the great tribulation through martyrdom.

The true virgin bride of Christ leaves the pagan religious traditions of her ancestors in favor of accepting Christ's hand in marriage. She is married to the bridegroom who purchased her hand in marriage on Calvary. Religious traditions have been left in the dustbin of her past.

She is on her way to the promised land where she will rule and reign in Christ's coming millennial kingdom for a thousand years.

RLTW
March 27, 2023

## Battlefield of the Mind

I was studying scripture and Bible history for hours on end as many of my friends were fighting in Afghanistan and other Muslim countries tracking down those responsible for the attacks in New York.

I had begun to focus my studies on the life of King David. Mary was promised that her son would sit upon the throne of David in Jerusalem for a thousand years. His throne would finally be among men, as Emmanuel once again would dwell with men.

The Bible has been separated by men into two Testaments. Jesus Christ labeled the word of God as a single sword with two edges. A warrior understands that both edges carry the same purposes and are equal in application in defeating the enemies of God.

I became a student willing to learn from God alone. The Bible stated that I received an anointing from God that is real, not counterfeit. I did not need any man to teach the things of God. First John

2:27 makes this biblical claim. How does that fare with ministry gifts?

Preachers, teachers, evangelists, and prophets are all titles many ascribe to claim. I realized very early in my ministry that it is God who is the source of biblical revelation. I might hear something from a man or woman that appears godly, but my responsibility as a child of God is to study scripture daily and rely on the mouth of at least two biblical witnesses to clear up matters of doctrine.

No scripture is available for individual interpretation. I began to realize that God conceived the Bible in a form of literature that was supernatural. The heptadic structure and the biblical prose of the Bible proves the Bible was conceived by God, and it was conceived completely outside of how humans experience time.

I began to experience a form of peace I had not achieved in my life for a long time, if ever. Then the Bush-Cheyney machine pushed a narrative that Iraq possessed nuclear weapons and chemical weapons that were bound for the hands of terrorists.

A second front was opened, and American sons and daughters would soon be dying in Iraq. I knew in my heart that the Cheyney family had only greed and dynasty in mind as my friends once again would be called upon to achieve goals political eugenicists held.

Dick Cheyney succeeded in forming the first ever American mercenary force. Rich people in America once again would benefit monetarily as poor children invaded Iraq to secure oil and gas revenues for the many American corporations the Cheyneys have their hands on.

You want to know why a Cheyney is on the January 6 committee? Look no further than the globalist agenda advanced by Dick Cheyney, a wolf dressed in sheep's clothing ever willing to sacrifice my friends in war to maintain his family's grip on the American federal budget.

By 2004, I had several friends who served with me during the 1990s now serving in Special Mission Units chasing the men who attacked us. Now they would be called upon to possibly die to keep one political family benefitting from the war being fought by American sons and daughters.

I had buried many friends by this stage of my life in cemeteries dotting the American landscape. I had now lost three friends who survived the battle of Mogadishu, only to succumb to demons and suck start their own pistols! I had enough of men's wars!

I began to contemplate why God saved me after being shot three times with an AK-47 on October 3, 1993. My life had been, for the most part, a complete trainwreck, and narcotics was how I dealt with the feelings of hopelessness. I wanted to grow old with these men.

January 1, 2004, saw me make a decision for God and any of my friends who might actually make it home from this protracted war the government was profiting from and had no intention of ending. I now had a responsibility to begin praying in earnest for my friends in harm's way.

Lucifer decided to try and derail what God had started on January 8, 2004. America lost an American hero, and I had lost my Christian brother Aaron Weaver in Iraq. If America only understood what made my friend Aaron tick!

Aaron was first and foremost an amazing friend. He wound up being an amazing father, an amazing husband, a great pilot, and a great American. And best of all, Aaron was a born-again believer in Jesus Christ.

Aaron had survived testicular cancer after finishing Flight School. He was serving as a reconnaissance pilot in Iraq with the Eighty-Second Airborne Division. He did not have to be there! He could have stayed on profile in the rear, home with his family. This was not Aaron's modus operandi.

I had learned in Somalia that Aaron would never sit at home while his men or his brothers in arms were in a fight! Aaron was a US Army Airborne Ranger who had been forged in the crucible of ground combat on the streets of Mogadishu, Somalia. He was a born leader!

I had planned to link up with Aaron in his retirement, just to hear the stories of his endearing life. I wanted to meet his children and see them grow up to be great human beings. God had other plans for my Ranger buddy. I had to focus my life on serving those coming home and their families left behind.

Christianity was never going to be the majority opinion. It was never supposed to be about comfort, but on the contrary, Christianity is best learned in the valleys of life. It is about empathy. Aaron is the greatest example of Christian empathy.

He knew he was no better or no worse than the men he led and fought beside. I believe Aaron was the best! His smile was unwavering. His courage was indomitable. His loyalty was unfettered. His love for Rangers cannot be understated. He is my Christian brother!

At his memorial, God gave me incredible peace. The still soft voice of God said, "Be still and know that I am God," as Taps was playing for the final time in my Ranger brother's life.

Jesus Christ reminded me that goodbyes are reserved for those who will never see each other again.

I will see Aaron on the other side of glory as he guides me to the mansion Jesus Christ has prepared for me in heaven and as he prepares to receive his soul winner's crown. Aaron caused me to question my beliefs, and for that I am eternally grateful. Thank you, Ranger buddy!

RLTW
March 28, 2023

## Christian Zionist

The year 2004 saw the inauguration of George Bush for a second term. Ross Perot's words to me way back in 1997 were coming true in my own life. "America will one day clamor for a viable third party with God's morality guiding their footsteps." Eugenics of the Republican kind on full display.

I had begun to discover my Jewish ancestors in immigration records overseas. Apparently, my biological mother was actually descended from Ukrainian Jews, not Polish Catholics. I began to study ancient Jewish manuscripts and the history of religion. Life was changing for me.

I had studied the book of Colossians. It ends with a command from Paul to redeem the time in our lives. I set out to understand and ask God how this is possible. My journey began with God whispering in my ear "Look to the times when you thought I was not God, and you will find me chasing you!"

I had become, at best, agnostic when I joined the Army. Religion held no sway over my members. Too much hypocrisy permeates the lives of denominational Christians. They left sound Old Testament teaching on absolute morality taught to my Jewish ancestors in favor of replacement theology, which claimed that the Jews lost their inheritance and God replaced them with Gentile believers.

This heresy makes God a liar. We indeed are not under the law unless we violate the law intentionally. Jesus Christ came to offer mercy and grace. They are who he is, not what he does! He is the good shepherd of his flock. His shepherd staff has two ends, eternal mercy and unwavering grace.

You cannot have one without the other. Mercy's keys alone unlock grace's door. The Old Testament is our example for what we need mercy from. Today, every single violation that occurred in Israel is now religious tradition in church. Believing grace covers willful acts of blaspheming God is preposterous.

I was done with church by 2004. God desired personal relationship to him over church attendance. I could take church into the world, and God intended to use my testimony to reach the men I admire the most: the American fighting man and woman!

The Bible I was reading told another story not being told in church, which puts to bed anti-Semitism in church. If Christians understood which Sabbaths Jesus Christ kept in his life and why, more people would be in church tonight!

Instead, Christians keep a Western solar calendar given by Constantine that purposely replaced God's Bible timeline with Roman pagan traditions that emigrated to Rome from Babylon.

The Roman Pope gave us Santa, Ishtar, Eros, Mother's Day, Father's Day, and birthdays. All are pagan traditions that scripture condemns. Can God overlook what he punished national Israel for doing first? The abandonment wrath of God has manifested, and America's crown is being replaced as I pen these words. Repent, for the kingdom of God is near!

When Christ appeared to open his ministry in Jerusalem, he confronted the priests. Their response was "We have Abraham our father." Ancestor worship became more important to the Jews than knowledge of the word of God. Religious traditions and legalism had taken hold in the temple.

Christ reminded them that they have only one father, which was God in heaven.

Who came to celebrate the birth of Jesus Christ, believers or unbelievers? Did the magi have a tradition learned from Daniel that pointed to Jesus Christ being born king of the Jews, who would save the world from their sins? Jews do not celebrate birthdays; it will violate the word of God.

Ecclesiastes 7:1 states, "It is better to celebrate the day of one's death, more than the day of one's birth."

Remember, Jesus Christ was the only baby ever born who knew the exact second he would give up the Ghost. His purpose for being born was to redeem mankind to God the Father by dying at the hands of those he created to worship him! Dying became the joy of his life.

For the joy that was set before him, Christ Jesus endured the cross. As I began to really comprehend the Bible narrative from the Jewish perspective, I realized we all had it wrong in America. Our eugenic upbringing allows us to believe in our hearts that unity is found in denominationalism.

The entire world is practicing syncretism, mixing the world order with religious piety, all having different versions of what the endgame is. I decided I would become a Christian Zionist because our story ends in the New Jerusalem. I began studying the Bible letter by letter.

I realized the body of Christ and national Israel have the same destiny but distinctly different paths on getting there. Both are entirely scriptural, and both determine how and when you will actually stand before God to give an account for those things having done with your testimony of saving faith in Jesus Christ.

As a Gentile, you can become the virgin bride of Christ by allowing the blood of the lamb to cover everything that does not line up with the Bible narrative. The purpose of the new birth is to create in all of us a clean heart and renew an upright spirit in us.

The cross of Christ is the most preposterous debt payment plan in human history—to have the God of creation allow his people to humiliate, mock, and crucify him, and all for the purpose of saving them from their own shortcomings.

Fulfilling the promise to Christians of a mansion in heaven, a kingdom on earth, where they co-rule with Christ in Jerusalem, as he fulfills the prophecy of the bema seat of judgment, coming down from heaven, and the sheep and goats judgment's beginning. Our crowns will be rewarded as we meet our risen bridegroom in heaven at the rapture.

We must pray for the nation of Israel. Pray for the peace of Jerusalem. Pray for revival in America.

Offer mercy to all we encounter. Only then will grace appear in the lives of those we love.

RLTW
March 28, 2023

## Go Ye into All the World

The great commission. A command from Jesus Christ given to his friends after his resurrection. What was the reaction of the first-century believers?

Paul the Apostle gives the most comprehensive definition of the Gospel in the New Testament. Paul is the most educated man in the New Testament. He is Jewish Rabbi, who was mentored in the law, the prophets, and the history of the nation of Israel.

His teacher was the most venerated rabbi in the Gentile world who was living and teaching out of the synagogue in Tarsus, the city of Paul's upbringing. Paul also enjoyed the benefits of a secular education, and he practiced a trade during his life that would provide for his flock.

Paul was uniquely qualified to teach Israel's future and the fledgling body of Christ's calling. Paul was the first-century equivalent of a genius. He spoke Hebrew, Greek, Latin, and the local dialect of the Syrian language. Paul was qualified to preach and teach sinners.

The persecutions of the first-century Jewish believers in Israel led to the ministry of Paul to the Gentile world. This was always God's plan. Not all have the courage to undergo persecution to the point of death for the testimony that Jesus Christ came to save us all from our sins.

Divisions between Jewish zealots and Gentile proselytes of Paul led to the spread of the Gospel into the Western Greek world, as persecution sent most believers running from Jerusalem. Paul identifies the Gospel in the book of 1 Corinthians 15.

Jesus Christ died according to scripture. Jesus Christ was buried according to scripture. Jesus Christ rose again the third day according to scripture. Which scripture did Paul have access to to make his claim as to the identity of the whole Gospel? Have Gentile Christians added to or taken away from Paul's gospel?

I began to contemplate doctrines of men in late 2004. I tried attending every denomination of Christian church. They are found on every corner in the America I love. I found all of them were violating the truths of the entire Bible, and I realized that denominational churches are, at best, anti-Semitic.

The first-century church of Ephesus had lost their first love. The apostles who could not wait to find Jesus each morning on the shores of Galilee were now more worried about building three-dimensional structures to mimic the pagan world littered with pagan temples.

The apostles' first love, as identified by Christ, was their desire to spend time alone with Christ as the living word of God. Today, nothing has changed in America. Believers are comfortable with two hours on Sunday and an hour on Wednesday while accepting Roman traditions as godly.

No one spends time alone with Jesus Christ in the study of scripture. Western denominations have adopted a Gospel of works as they add water baptism, speaking in tongues, and outward piety as measures of a Christian testimony. You must not be Christian if you do not believe like us!

A modern hostage crisis has taken place in denominational churches, and God wants to be released into the world to once again save sinners from their own shortcomings. Judgment in church has replaced unending mercy offered by Christ from Calvary.

The year 2005 began for me in Decatur, Georgia, where I had begun to share my faith in Jesus Christ on train platforms, as well as on Megabus journeys to spend time with my Ranger brothers coming home from war. I had concluded that the world is seeking a savior; it was time to offer them mine.

I chose to focus on what Christ was offering me every morning. I knew my flesh was hopelessly corrupt. Christianity had totally become about what Christ was accomplishing in my own life, despite my continued reliance on methadone. Patience was the lesson God was teaching me.

I had begun to ask God for biblical revelation of the truths on why Christ had to die. I realized that the Crucifixion was not the tragedy church was presenting. On the contrary, the Crucifixion was the plan of the Trinity of creation. It was the most preposterous debt payment plan in human history.

The only way to earn the forgiveness of sin was to acknowledge that I am chief among sinners. This was Paul's testimony, and in 2005, it became my testimony. From this time forward, I would never judge anyone else again! I would look in the mirror of scripture and allow the Holy Spirit to chasten me to truth.

I began to understand that the Bible is a supernatural book conceived entirely outside of how humans experience time. This was profound, as God began to use my science brain to reveal his Son as the creator of the universe.

With this revelation, I could begin to experience peace after returning from war, completely changed. My innocence was lost in five hours one sunny Sunday afternoon in Mogadishu, Somalia. A very young boy had to become a man, in one gunfight! The next thirty years became a testimony of finding peace.

I had read in scripture that Jesus Christ is the prince of peace as his inheritance from God the Father. My peace was found in the knowledge that Christ alone can overcome all that was plaguing me as a professed believer. Christ had to become my overcomer; I had to just believe!

The Gospel of Jesus Christ is a transforming message. God begins to align your spirit and soul with your actions in the flesh over time. You indeed become a new creation, and the individual witness should be one of you and I showing eternal mercy from Christ with all that we encounter.

The Crucifixion was the ultimate gift from God. It is most misunderstood. A gift is best received when it is shared freely. Your redemption was paid for by the death of the only begotten Son of God. Now I have the privilege of sharing this truth with all God places in my path.

RLTW
March 29, 2023

## Surrender Is Not a Ranger Word

To ascribe to becoming an Airborne Ranger has more unknowns than those things which are obvious. The Ranger creed is where men make a promise to their nation and the Ranger on their left and right.

I would be lying if I said I understood what went into being a Ranger. What I now know from hindsight is that when you get past the external and begin to understand what makes Rangers tick, no greater human can be found on earth.

The man under the beret and behind the badges is extremely human. Bravado is his calling, while humility is his watchword. It is the humble Rangers who learn empathy in duress that change communities. Surrender has become achievable in my own life.

This is very counterintuitive, for we promise to never surrender even if I am the last man alive to defend old glory! Who and what a Ranger surrenders to becomes a blessing or a curse to those around him.

117

The Ranger creed is most often recited. It was not until after Mogadishu that I began to contemplate, *Am I the man found in the creed?* The jury is still out, but I have learned a couple of lessons from my Ranger mentors along this journey.

First, the lessons I learned from the men I was given the chance to follow and lead daily as a Ranger leader still serve me today. I cut my teeth in B3/75. Weapons Platoon and Third Platoon are where I learned Ranger life. The men under me deserve all the credit for who I have become.

Empathy is to understand you are no better or no worse off than those you lead and serve. Daily Ranger life requires physical and spiritual strength, best learned in hardship. Every great Ranger lesson is learned in the valleys of life, on the way to every mountain-top objective.

My Ranger squad in Somalia was awesome, each man with strengths and weaknesses understood by all. Learning to share each load is the key to Ranger success. The Ranger buddy system ensures we have a chance to come good on the creed, when bullets start flying and bombs start dropping.

Third Platoon drew a tough mission that has gotten lost in a narrative. We drew the Ranger mission of supplying the vehicle blocking force. It was our primary responsibility to keep our enemy at bay. No one gets into the objective, and no one gets out.

Our secondary mission was to assume responsibility of the prisoners and escort them back to our base. All of this had to be accomplished while under incredible enemy fire. Our vehicles were hopelessly trapped in a fatal funnel, from where the enemy focused their eighteen-hour assault.

While uploading prisoners, the first helicopter was shot down. At this point, we had to change missions to a recovery mission as every Ranger understood we were not returning to base without our wounded aviators and crew. Our brothers would be rescued, regardless of circumstances.

Enemy fire intensified as elements of the ground force who initially inserted began moving on foot toward where we believed the bird had gone down. Moving toward the gunfire was the hallmark of Ranger life. This is why our motto is "Rangers lead the way!"

My first gut punch came when over the radio, it was announced that Dominic Pilla was killed escorting our wounded brother back to the airfield. He was killed while firing on his killer. I miss Dominic every day. He was the best machine gunner in B Company, and all were great!

By this time in the fight, I had my .50-caliber gunner, Clay, who had a serious gunshot wound to his arm. Lorenzo immediately took over his job on the .50-caliber. This decision proved fatal. Lorenzo epitomized "Never shall I fail my comrades."

My machine gunner Dave Ritchie and I had been wounded by shrapnel. I was conversing with Staff Sergeant Dave Wilson when an enemy grenade exploded in the street, injuring him and me. Dave Ritchie never missed a single beat and continued to fight for the next eighteen-plus hours.

Next came our extremely heroic medic, John Stansfield, who took a bullet to his helmet that temporarily knocked him unconscious. Miraculously, he would awake and continue to treat my wounded men for the duration of the fight.

I would witness such incredible heroism by young Rangers that sunny Sunday afternoon. My fight would last approximately four-and-a-half hours. I would be shot three more times. If you want to know why I am here, I can only testify through writing about Jesus Christ's plans for my life.

The average age of the members of my squad was twenty-one years and six months. These are the American sons who came good on a promise to our citizenry and to me, as they alone kept me alive in Somalia.

Leadership is the principle of getting others to accomplish your mission by providing a purpose, a direction, and the motivation to accomplish the heroic. What I learned on October 3, 1993, is that each man was proving that the Ranger leadership model is working to keep America free.

Each member of my weapons squad is, in his own right, an American hero!

Why do I now serve the community that gave me so much in life? It is simple. The men who came before me and the Rangers I had the fortune of leading in ground combat are owed everything, including someone to help them find peace.

Every member of my weapons squad who survived Mogadishu went on to serve again in combat for the next twenty-eight years! This is why I serve!

I am old now, and surrender to me occurs each morning as I hit my knees and ask God for eternal mercy over my life and the men of Task Force Ranger. *Surrender* can become a Ranger word when the prince of peace is how you learn to find peace after returning from war!

RLTW
March 31, 2023

## The Reprobate Mind

As my journey meandered down the narrow path leading to my eventual salvation, I began to question what I was seeing in the America I had been willing to defend with my life. Christian nationalism would become my path forward. The two-edged sword of God's word would order every step.

I had now experienced divorce, and I was married for a second time. Was God happy?

The Bible says God hates divorce. He had framed civilization at creation. His plan was for one man to be with one woman for life. They were to reproduce and raise godly offspring. Those offspring were to be introduced to the word of God as soon as they were weaned from the breast and taken from the milk.

Train up a child in the way they should go, and when they are old, they will not depart from it.

My father had divorced my biological mother when I was an infant. The seeds planted would produce a harvest in my life as I, too, divorced my first wife and mother to my daughter.

After leaving home to travel to California for my first military assignment, I had found a beautiful young girl to spend my time with. Mona and I were inseparable for about three years as I began to plan for the rest of my life and a military career.

After returning from Ranger School and attending Primary Leadership Development Course in October 1989, Mona became pregnant. I had already decided to leave California and become a member of the Seventy-Fifth Ranger Regiment. My reporting date was January 1990 to attend Airborne School.

I would leave Mona in California as a pregnant nineteen-year-old with an amazing family to support her. I had no loyalty except to myself! I had never been introduced to the absolute morality in scripture; now I felt entitled to sexual intercourse without repercussions.

Mona would eventually visit me at Fort Benning as I began my service in B3/75 Ranger. She was much more mature than I. I was entertaining the notion that she should move to Georgia with our son. She could see that my loyalty was to myself and my career. She declined my invitation.

She would spend the next eighteen years raising my son, Andrew, who turned out to be a much better father than me. My son, Andrew, has five children of his own. An example of love for children taught by his mother, all alone. He is now serving in the Air Force and raising his own family. This is all because of his mother!

I would eventually meet my son at his base in South Carolina. He would visit me at my house in Georgia. I could tell that he was his mother's boy. I feel he could tell that I was struggling to find peace in life. My prayer is that God will somehow give me the courage to learn from Andrew how to be a grandparent.

Mona would marry and have seven more beautiful children. They understand service to a cause greater than themselves, and two of her daughters and two of her sons now serve in uniform. I believe Mona's dad, Carlos Bedolla, played a pivotal role in raising my son to become a good man.

I had now been married to Susan for four years. It was 2005, and we had a granddaughter about to come into the world, and I was very scared. I did not even understand the responsibility of fatherhood, and now a baby girl was to be born to my stepdaughter.

We received devastating news in December 2004, that the baby was developing irregularly and she would be born with hypoplastic left heart syndrome. In layman's terms, she would only have two heart valves. They recommended an abortion.

I could not be prouder of Susan's daughter as she resiliently said, "No, I will raise her no matter what the condition." The courage that decision took has caused me to admire my wife for raising her daughter in a way that was amazing. No selfishness anywhere in their lives.

Lillian Corryn Wolfenbarger was born on April 13, 2005. She would be on a medevac flight to a children's hospital within four minutes of being born. I prayed for God to give me the courage to become a father to Lisa, a husband to my wife, and a grandfather to Lillian. I was in uncharted waters!

Lillian would spend the first four months of her life undergoing two more open-heart surgeries. I spent my time split between the intensive care unit at a children's hospital in Atlanta and home preparing to welcome Lillian whenever the doctors said she was safe in our house.

God began teaching me to love unconditionally each time I held that baby while in intensive care. My heart was once again softening to the things of God. If I was ever going to become the man God intended, this little compromised baby was how God intended to restore my ability to parent.

Lisa would need help in raising Lillian. The baby's father was dealing with his own shortcomings. I prayed for Allen often to receive the peace of Jesus Christ. For now, we had to learn to adapt to focus on giving this wonderful gift from God as normal a life as possible.

I was confronting my life biblically. I realized I had violated the first covenant in the Bible found in Genesis 2:24. One man with one woman for life, raising godly offspring. Now I had a chance to influence a baby girl who was not even my biological child. I needed God's word more than ever.

I realized our society was now violating every covenant in scripture. God has turned our society over to a reprobate mind.

Homosexuality is the curse God released on America for legislating the Bible and prayer out of our children's lives.

This is hard to swallow for believers who want to blame homosexuals. God's desire is to offer them eternal mercy. It is the Christian job to return to loving those we do not agree with. We will never know if God's desire to save them outweighs our desire to judge them until we do what Jesus would not do!

Jesus Christ would not judge the sinner while offering mercy. He would condemn sin on the cross and offer sinners only eternal mercy until he returns in the clouds.

Blessed are the merciful, for they shall be shown mercy!

*He was crucified upon a cross of wood, yet he*
*created the hill upon which it stood.*
*He is alive forevermore, and he is returning*
*for his virgin bride very soon.*

RLTW
March 30, 2023

# THE TENNESSEE RIVER, CHATTANOOGA

The year 2007 began with a decision by my wife to leave work and, as a family, we would focus on raising Lillian together. She was growing and becoming quite the entertainer. Her smile was contagious.

We wanted a new beginning for Lisa, and my wife and I always felt like country living suited us better.

We began taking road trips north on 75 headed toward Chattanooga, Tennessee. We would purchase a Nissan Titan. Now we were on the hunt for a little piece of land with an old house to remodel for our family.

Our journeys always began with a newspaper and property for sale. We probably searched in four counties before finding land and a house we could pay cash for. Unfortunately, I was still on methadone, so our choices involved land near a methadone clinic.

We settled on Chickamauga, Georgia, where we purchased 2.9 acres with a house in terrible condition. Nonetheless, it was livable for the time being as we settled in to life in Rossville, Georgia. We began making friends immediately, whom we cherish still.

I decided this was where I would get off the methadone. I met with my counselor who agreed to allow me to detox by reducing my dose by five milligrams each week to ensure success. This process of detox would take me a little over a year. I returned to the Veterans Administration for outpatient care.

North Georgia provided an opportunity to rendezvous with a Ranger buddy from my squad in Mogadishu. Ernest Sandy Pursley from Ringgold, Georgia, is the squad member that quite possibly helped me with the most mischief in my life.

He lived about twelve miles from me. I lived there for eighteen months before I realized he was back home in beautiful Catoosa County, Georgia. It was late 2008, and it was almost as like it were June of 1993, kids reuniting after not seeing each other for seventeen years.

Every decision from this day forward would begin with "Hold my beer!" The really good decisions most often began with "Watch this shit!" Needless to say, my poor wife would make more than one trip to Walker County Jail and Erlanger Hospital after a day of drinking and breaking an ankle while riding with Sandy.

I had begun to attend a veteran group at the Chattanooga Veterans Center. My counselor was Chuck Ayers, a fellow Purple Heart recipient and born-again Christian. His empathy ensured that only God was capable of judging men. Chuck accepted me with my bumps and bruises.

The Vet Center became a place of solace and retreat for me. I became comfortable enough to begin running my own Bible study class hosted by my friend and counselor, Chuck Ayers. This brought the scrutiny of his peers, and soon I felt our Bible study could not be tolerated as a matter of law.

This devastated me. I was home from war, experiencing a strong delusion of peace, and the people assigned to help me find peace set out to destroy a tool in my rapidly expanding toolbox that they had first encouraged me to create to successfully overcome addiction.

I became more obsessive in my study of scripture. I lost hope in the Veterans Administration system as anything more than a failing socialist model with veterans as the test dummies.

To think the God who brought me home from war and the God who brought my Vietnam brothers home from war would now not be allowed to help us find elusive peace. Our nation had lost focus, and now I was determined to find out when.

I began spending hours watching Chuck Missler of Koinonia Institute to replace narcotics. I finally became addicted to something that would help make sense of my entire life. I spent days on end never eating, sleeping, or showering while watching Dr. Missler's presentation of the Bible.

I watched every commentary on every book of the Bible I could find on YouTube at least three times each over the next fifteen years of daily Bible study. Dr. Missler opened my eyes to the present reality facing believers and unbelievers.

Through his ministry, God revealed to me that the entire Bible was conceived entirely outside of how humans experience time! I had already been studying the Hebrew Old Testament letter by letter; now I began to understand the Greek New Testament through the eyes of history.

I spent much of this year incapacitated by two injuries: broken ribs after falling through a barn roof and then a broken ankle in the fall while riding shotgun with Sandy on Aetna Mountain in Chattanooga. This occurred on the way up the mountain. Made no sense to leave till the party ended.

Sandy would deposit me in the emergency room while escaping the wrath of Susan, my wife. I had managed to get to the hospital with a blood alcohol level of .23. Fireball is not recommended when good decisions about riding on four-wheelers are abreast.

This year, while trying to deal with my previous addiction leading to horrible decision-making as a pattern in my life, I began consuming alcohol in copious amounts on binge opportunities. Mostly when I would hang out with Sandy for a day, that most often turned into a three-day bender.

But on one occasion, I decided to bushhog the property we had purchased. We had been living in a town home in Chickamauga. We had fenced in the back field, and Susan had purchased a horse for her and Lillian to enjoy.

The property turned into a gathering place. On this day, I would be joined by my neighbor, Bobby, a much older man who enjoyed a drink of shine every now and again. He met me in the yard at 8:30 a.m. We would both pass out after consuming two quarts.

Susan finally heard from me as I crashed my car into a drainage culvert, and my German shepherd and I were running from the deputies who had a roadblock set up less than 1,000 yards from where I deposited my wife's car. Now my German shepherd and I were fugitives.

This lasted for an hour as he and I exited the woods in front of the sheriff. I sat down in the road in front of his patrol vehicle, at which time he asked me if I was driving the cutlass on Long Hollow Road. My response brought immediate action by the deputy: "No, my dog was driving!"

You might think this ended up bad, but the rest of this story is best told around a campfire. This incident brought me closer to Christ when I realized when God calls you for his purposes and you believe he died to pay the only debt that matters when I die, nothing can separate you from his love!

RLTW
April 4, 2023

## An American Tragedy

I have shared my testimony of addiction often. I have questioned my nation's commitment to winning the drug war. Narcotics can be found in every neighborhood in America. The consumption mentality has paralyzed the prison industrial complex. America's answer to addiction is incarceration.

Our legal system seems to function best when large quantities of people are incarcerated, on parole, probation, or some other form of community monitoring. No family has been spared. Generations struggle with the paralysis of narcotic abuse.

Train up a child in the way they should go, and when they are old, they will not depart from it. I have found this paradigm applies to teaching both good and bad things. Our children want nothing more than to be like us. It applies to addiction as well.

I was addicted for most of my own daughter's upbringing. She has now struggled with her own addiction nightmare. I have asked God for mercy over her life and my own. I planted seeds that have transferred to her own life. My message to her is, God is sovereign. He alone can deliver us from the stronghold of addiction.

When Lillian finally left the hospital, she came home to live with me, my wife, and her mother. Lillian's father had been incarcerated because of activity stemming from addiction to methamphet-amine. Allen was a good kid. I tried to be a steadying voice as he dealt with his demons.

The beginning of 2009 saw our family trying to give Lillian as normal a life as possible. Her mother and Allen had moved into their own apartment. We shared babysitting duties as they both were working. Life seemed to be normal on the surface.

As we prepared to celebrate Lilian's birthday, tragedy struck home. Allen's demons had caught up to him, as he would be killed by a man he thought was his friend. Together they entered a service station, and the man he was with decided to brandish a shotgun to rob the attendant.

Something occurred between Allen and his accomplice when he turned the gun on Allen and fired. He bled to death on the floor of a gas station, killed by his own accomplice. The man would be caught three days later in Mississippi and extradited to Decatur for prosecution.

It was March 12, 2009. Death had plagued my existence surrounding drug addiction. Acquaintances of mine were overdosing, all the while I was losing friends from Task Force Ranger to war and suicide way too often. Losing six Rangers in war has not hurt as bad as hearing of the seven who have taken their own lives after surviving war.

I understand what it takes to prosecute war. I wish our government did as well. The drug war is no different. The narrative surrounding our retreat from Afghanistan is the culmination of the inability of elected officials to stomach victory in war. The drug war is being won by cartels.

I have drawn the conclusion that politicians need narcotics to help them create a class system. I believe our elected officials understand that people addicted means prisons can be built and a deplorable class of American must be fed narcotics to keep the prison industrial complex rolling.

America has the technology to win the drug war decisively. It would not take long, and our neighbors in Mexico to the south could have their corrupt government weeded out. That is not the plan. The plan is to aid cartels in order to change the voting demographics.

Our government is on a global trajectory. Elected officials are practicing class eugenics, and narcotics are the tool employed to deal with the deplorable class. The sociopolitical elite class desires to control education, entertainment, news, commerce, thought, and religion.

They are waging a global war that has aided the rise of China. As a warfighter, it seems they have orchestrated this Asian takeover. How many Americans realize Joe Biden served in Congress when Richard Nixon hosted the first Chinese premier in 1973?

It was at this time that socialists formed a plan to liquidate America's industrial manufacturing base and give it to China. Poor neighborhoods became drug markets in every major city where jobs are scarce. This is a carefully devised global plan emanating from the world economic forum.

The elected officials in the Democratic Party hate nationalism. Their desire is to be the ruling class that alone prospers while we accept government scraps. Stuck in the middle are the millions of hardworking people required to work to feed the government tax machine.

Joe Biden has not paid for fuel, food, travel, clothing, or lodging for forty-five years. You wonder why he says life is good; it's because you and I have subsidized his life for a long time. He has no ability to show empathy toward ordinary American struggles because he has never faced them and he sees us as deplorable and stupid!

Eugenics requires an ultra-rich class of racists from every color and persuasion of humanity. They hide in plain sight reminding us how racist we are. They should be able to identify racism; it stares them in their own faces each time they look in the mirror.

Their eugenic master is our current president who despises the poor class of Americans he continues to court in elections. No one has been hurt more by Biden policies than the African American community that continues to place him and other eugenicists in office.

The Democratic Party has unleashed their plan to end patriotism and nationalism in America. Globalism ensures they alone will prosper from American toil. Immigration of poor Hispanics and other nationalities of the poor to America is part of their plan to seize power for good.

Look for an executive order giving citizenship to illegals before the 2024 election. Joe Biden realizes his time is short. He realizes the Black vote means nothing in the future because poor Americans, both Black and White, are being replaced to keep them in power eternally.

Narcotics are their gift to poor Americans who come from places where the Democrats manufactured the destruction of America's ability to prosper. Their goal is godlessness!

Only the blood of the Lamb of God can save America now! Jesus Christ is the only way America remains great!

RLTW
April 1, 2023

## Chickamauga, Georgia

Susan and I began spending a lot of time at the northwest Georgia battlefield with Lillian and Lisa. I had purchased books on the battle, and the grounds are incredibly inspiring. I would spend countless hours engrossed in reading the plaques and dreaming of the combatants' horrifying battle.

Life in north Georgia had become less chaotic than city living. We had moved over to a town house a few miles from our property as Susan reenrolled in college. I was happy she was enjoying the pursuit of her degree. She had placed her children's future ahead of her own early in life.

This was her chance to fulfill a life dream. She had already been extremely successful in her own right over her professional career. She had achieved the status of mortgage bank vice president when she and I met. Now she and I could focus on Lisa and Lillian.

I was successfully navigating my detox from methadone. I had met new acquaintances and often helped them on projects at their homes to kill time. In my life, the idle mind indeed becomes the devil's workshop. My time in north Georgia ended up no different.

I returned to the Veterans Administration health care toward the end of my detox. I had suffered an injury of three fractured ribs after falling through a two-story metal roof, directly onto the horse stall below. The impact felt like nothing I had ever experienced.

The hydrocodone ran out, so I asked my primary care doctor for pain management help. I now found myself on morphine sulfate and oxycodone. Methadone was a thing of my past, but I fell back into addiction relapse after injury. I had a lot of time in a recliner to contemplate.

I engrossed myself in Bible study and discussions about life with all who would listen. Even in my valley of relapse, God was somehow changing how I saw salvation in Christ. He was proving he was sovereign over the affairs of men. I realized I could not sin my way out of his eternal mercy.

If God is indeed sovereign and we are indeed finite, is the gulf between God's righteousness and our fallibility just too great for religion and tradition to bridge? I had a stronghold that has plagued my existence since birth. I learned it from my mother and father: addiction to pharmaceuticals.

I decided one day after almost overdosing to present myself to the VA emergency room in Murfreesboro for the purpose of immediate detox. I wanted off narcotics, and I knew withdrawals at this point needed medical monitoring.

I was insistent that I wanted a cold-turkey detox, no psychiatric medications or weaning. I was sick, and I was tired. Until an addict becomes sick and tired of being perpetually sick and perpetually tired, the black muddy river keeps rolling on forever. Only Christ can overcome strongholds!

After Allen's death, his mother moved in with us at our town-home. I enjoyed Madolyn at this time, for she was grieving the loss of her son while getting to spend a whole lot of time with her grand-daughter. She and I both began to discuss our faith often and reading Lillian the Bible.

It was refreshing being able to experience grief with people I loved and respected. It had been a long time since I had been around my brothers in arms to toast our fallen. I was finding a family at home during the deepest and darkest valley of my life. God met me in the valley!

It is in the valleys of life where rivers meander. They seem to provide so many answers to all of life's questions: washing, refreshing, meandering, changing, supplying, destroying, but eternally constant. This is the conundrum in life best understood when God is navigating our journey.

Northwest Georgia became a lecture hall from God. Every human experience I would spend listening and learning from other people's struggles while never judging. The friends I met in Chickamauga were descended from people whose entire existence was forged in hardship.

Lillian had started school at the local Baptist academy. I loved the thought of a Christian education if it focused on the mercy and grace of the Bible message. Lillian enjoyed getting to sing and dance for Jesus Christ at school, and that is what mattered.

During this time, my relationship with Bob Gallagher was rekindled. He had made the decision to retire, and he was moving to Savannah. He wanted us to link up as soon as possible, once he resettled his family. All were looking forward to getting home and retiring with Bob, who deserved peace.

We talked in length about how we were going to serve veterans. I shared my faith in what I was reading in the Bible. I told him about building a home for a severely disabled veteran in north Georgia and how I was joining a class of veterans in Chattanooga once a week for fellowship.

We looked forward to linking back up and celebrating Bob's life as a true American hero.

Bob Gallagher was my platoon sergeant in Mogadishu, only after jumping into Panama with Alpha 3/75 on the Rio Hata Airfield. He went on to earn a Silver Star and subsequent Purple Heart in the taking of Baghdad. Bob was filmed getting shot at the Baghdad airport.

If heroism is indeed a valued trait in leadership, Bob held it in oodles. Under pressure, no one was calmer. Wounded or not, Bob was cool under duress. Humility was pondered at every question.

Bob was empathetic to the daily grind as Rangers for he had done it for a long time.

I so looked ahead to a reunion with my mentor. It was not meant to be. I received the news Bob had suffered a massive heart attack a few days after speaking to him in the kitchen of the home where his incredible life ended. It was October 2014, and I was again devastated by a loss.

Faith in Christ guided me through another valley toward the mountaintop of eternity.

RLTW
April 10, 2023

## Behind the Veil

The moniker of my nonprofit and title for my first book has become my window to the heart and mind of God. Learning to become a virgin bride has been the most humbling experience of my life. The Bible narrative is most misunderstood without the teaching about Christ's reward and inheritance.

Jesus Christ was promised both while in the womb of Mary. His inheritance was a future kingdom, seated on David's throne in Jerusalem. His reward is a virgin bride taken from all nations, peoples, and tongues. The last two thousand years, God has been offering men Christ's hand in marriage.

The Old Testament is where we are intended to learn the stories of biblical men and women who learned mercy through disobedience. When God loves you, he is required to chasten you. This chastening comes in the form of his permissive will.

His permissive will is on display in Job 1 when God calls Lucifer to heaven to give account on where he has been and what he has been doing. God is sovereign over evil as well as good. He allows the shining one to sow chaos in our lives when disobedience requires mercy and love.

On the cross of Calvary, the veil of the earthly tabernacle was rent in two. Men had placed more faith in the holiness of the temple than they had faith or relationship to the God who sanctified the temple. The created things had become more important than relationship to their creator.

God desires personal fellowship. Anything that leads to you spending less time with God reminds God he is less important to you. Lucifer seizes opportunities to disrupt our relationship to Jesus by sowing death, hell, and the grave when our prayer life is lacking.

Prayer is God's way of enlisting believers to get involved in what he is already doing. By not praying often, we lose sight of what is most important to God, which is children learning how to be in relationship to Jesus Christ.

We had enrolled Lillian in private Christian preschool. I felt she needed more time home with us, and public school seemed like a good option in January of 2013. Lillian met new friends. However, she was missing praising and dancing to Jesus Christ with her friends at the Baptist academy.

We were enjoying more time with her as her days were shorter, and she could enter and leave the bus from our driveway. Life seemed very normal for the little girl who had endured so much in her budding six-year-old existence. She and I became inseparable when she was not in school.

Susan was settling in to her new life being educated at Dalton State College. Madolyn was working a few different jobs and helping with raising and enjoying time spent with Lillian. Lisa was working and doing what twenty-something single mothers do. I was enjoying learning to redeem time.

We all were staying involved in Lillian's health and welfare. Field trips became family functions. We began making many trips to the Tennessee River for festivals and great food. Walking along the river and watching an innocent child dance and play was refreshing. I was learning to love again.

How many of us truly understand the majesty and sovereignty of God the creator? Can we indeed learn the character of a loving creator in comfort, or is his love best experienced in restoration after hardship? My testimony is one where I did not realize how much God loved me until I truly grasped sovereignty.

I had to surrender to his control completely if I intended to recover from addiction and learn the heart and mind of God. *Surrender* had to become a Ranger word. I was failing at getting myself completely free of narcotics. It was taking a toll on my family relationships, including Lillian.

On March 13, 2023, Susan walked Lillian to the bus to send her off to school. It was the first warm day of the coming spring after a cold winter. Lisa, Susan, and I were all home that day. We all eagerly awaited the bus to bring Lillian home.

As the bus pulled to our curb, Lillian sprinted onto the porch straight past Susan to inquire of me if she could please play outside. Susan decided she needed to change her shoes to outdoor shoes for playing. Lillian hastily donned her shoes and headed to the play area where her friends were all playing.

I was seated on the porch reading a newspaper when Lillian and her friend presented themselves with a pain issue in Lillian's ankle. I petitioned her to come sit on Yo-Yo's lap. As she pointed out from where her pain was radiating, her eyes rolled up in her head, and she aspirated.

I lifted her in my arms and kicked our door open to ask my now-screaming wife and daughter to please calm down and call an ambulance. I proceeded to clear her airway and begin chest compressions and artificial breathing. She was not responding. I began to ask God for mercy over her young life.

The ambulance arrived and proceeded to whisk her to Erlanger Hospital. We loaded up in Susan's car for the ride that changed our entire existence. Somehow, God settled me in the moment to calm my wife and daughter. I knew she was gone! The question remained: "What now?"

As we entered the hospital, we were met by staff and a chaplain. They informed us that they tried everything, but it seems she threw a blood clot that claimed her compromised life. The tears of my wife and daughter were breaking my heart. I prayed for courage from God.

A doctor came to see me with a request. There was a little girl going blind who could be helped if we donated Lillian's corneas.

Now I know why God had me ask for courage. In a minute, I would have to ask my bereaved daughter and my wife to give someone else the gift of sight.

I needed the peace of God more than ever in my life.

RLTW
April 10, 2023

# Jeremiah 29:11

One month shy of her seventh birthday, we prepared to bury our granddaughter. *Devastated* is an understatement. A memorial was being planned to occur in three days. The Christian school she attended offered the auditorium to accommodate her service.

Neither I nor my wife ate a thing over the next three days. Decisions had to be made about speakers to eulogize Lillian. The question arose whether we should allow the pastor to deliver a sermon. I said, "We have time. Let me pray about this important decision."

Before leaving Lillian at the hospital, Lisa and Susan had cut off a few of her beautiful, curly blond locks. Susan gripped them as her, and I sat paralyzed on our living room couch. We dreaded visitors, and there were many I never expected. God proved Lillian had moved many people in her short life.

Many of the nice people from the Baptist church delivered food and cold drinks over the next few days. I was contemplating who should deliver a sermon. The Spirit revealed it had to be me. I would ask God for the message he intended for me to deliver.

As clear as day, I heard the still, soft voice of God whispering, "Goodbyes are reserved for those you will never see again." If we could summon the courage to believe Jesus Christ is in control, we would see Lillian again. I was hurting and asking God, "Why?" I realized this was extremely selfish. Lillian belonged to Jesus Christ, and I needed to focus on how all of us can join her in eternity.

I had learned a biblical principle based upon how God sees the innocent. Lillian was completely innocent. She will inherit eternity with Pharaoh's firstborn. Lillian was under God's mercy. Right now, she is seated in the bosom of God in heaven, waiting on us to get there.

I tried to open my Bible to see what God had planned for my eulogy and sermon. Lillian would want Yo-Yo to teach the Bible, exactly as I did with her almost daily. She prayed on her knees like no child I have known. I now try to pray as often as her and, on my knees, when I remember.

Over the first two days, I just could not summon the strength to study. I just kept weeping and asking God for mercy in Jesus Christ. I kept reminding him I needed a word. Again, I heard his still, soft voice, "Those that wait upon the Lord shall renew their strength!"

On the third day, which was the morning of the memorial, I got on my knees. I needed the mercy and grace of God on this day more than most. I prayed the psalm: "May the words of my mouth and the meditation of my heart, be acceptable in thy sight, O Lord, my strength and my redeemer."

I still did not know exactly what God intended me to share, and I needed it in a few hours' time. I opened my Bible to the book of Jeremiah, for he is the weeping prophet. My heart carried me to chapter 29. As I began to read out loud, I reached verse 11: "For I know the thoughts I have toward you, thoughts of peace, and an expected end." God had settled it in my heart that although this was terrible, restoration has a purpose, and it is grounded in his love.

The pain all of us were feeling would be temporary. We would have the chance to see Lillian by remaining faithful to the knowledge that God is in control and Lillian is looking at us from God's bosom. It was her time to go home to meet the Jesus we all tried to introduce her too.

I had completely leaned on Christ for mercy and grace at a time when the fleshly John would seek solace in narcotics. My relationship to Christ was becoming completely real. Christ was once again opening the mouth of a jackass to reach those coming home from war.

Life is best experienced knowing my sin debt has been paid by Christ on Calvary. To believe life gets easier and struggles disappear was not what I was experiencing in my Christian walk. If anything, I was really experiencing an immense valley that would not disappear.

I began to compare my life to the hamster-in-the-cage mentality. The hamster gets on that wheel over and over again, fully knowing he will be back where he started and he will have gotten nowhere, yet he gets on the wheel. He becomes a creature of habit.

He understands that if I just let him out of that cage once, I will never see him again. This is addiction. If you can ever settle it in your mind that life sucks, but it sucks worse by relapsing, you got it whooped. Tools are best when used.

Lillian's death brought me to my knees. I figure God needed me returning to prayer and meditation. I began studying the Bible for hours on end. I began to contemplate my future serving God and veterans. My Christian walk would require segregation in prayer and fasting.

Susan and I moved out of our apartment by staying in various hotels throughout the Chattanooga area. Susan managed to remain in college. I would read the Bible and hang out with friends. Eventually we moved in with our friend. His basement became our self-imposed dungeon.

This lasted for a while out of convenience. Eventually I would answer a phone call from my Ranger buddy that has changed my stars. Once again, empathy was on display as Dave Floyd invited me to participate in an upcoming Special Operations Wounded Warriors' hogg hunt.

Susan talked me into it, and off to South Carolina I proceeded. The date was March of 2016.

Christ was moving in ways I could not have anticipated.

*He was crucified upon a cross of wood, yet he*
*created the hill upon which it stood.*
*He is alive forevermore, and he is returning*
*for his virgin bride very soon.*

RLTW
April 10, 2023

# THE PEE DEE RIVER, SOUTH CAROLINA

America had been at war with militant Islam for a sustained period of fifteen years by 2016. My knowledge of the Bible had led me to believe war will never end until Christ returns to set up his kingdom. As long as Israel is in the land and prospering, Islam will wage war.

All biblical prophecy goes through the nation of Israel and those nations that persecute Israel. America will one day turn on national Israel and seal our fate as an empire. The United Nations is now completely united in stopping God's plan to place Jesus Christ on David's throne in Jerusalem.

The sword shall never depart from the house of David until Shiloh comes. Shiloh is an Old Testament illusion to Jesus Christ's return after Israel looks upon him whom they have pierced and cry, "Hosanna, blessed is he who comes in the name of Adonai Elohim."

I had not been around my Ranger buddies unless we were attending funerals. This invitation would provide an opportunity to rendezvous with Ranger brothers from B3/75 whom I had not seen in years. The air of anticipation brought my adrenaline level to dizzying heights.

I had hunted squirrels in Ohio with my Ranger buddy Rick twenty years prior. I deer-hunted while at Ranger battalion with a few brothers. But truthfully, I have only ever been good at hunting two-legged prey. The majority of my adult life had been spent chasing our enemies and skirts.

To hunt wild hoggs sounded like an excuse to drink a whole lot, laugh a whole lot, and hang out with great dogs, and getting to stab a pig that is screaming sounded therapeutic. I prepared to fly to Myrtle Beach out of Chattanooga in March.

I would be gathered from the airport by my Ranger buddy Dave. It was great to see him doing very well. He had made the decision to start SOWW with a few buddies serving in Special Mission Units and a few civilians looking to support our nation's finest war fighters.

A quick stop at Bass Pro Shop to gather wet-weather gear, and then on to Tabor City, North Carolina, and Lays Lake for a week of hogg slaying and partying like it's 1999. I was introduced to my fellow hunters who all had been injured doing special things for our nation.

I also was introduced to coffee moonshine, which ended up being my friend and foe over the next week. I was awake drunk for over seventy-two hours. It was incredible to begin meeting men who had served our nation in the finest Special Operations units ever formed. These men had years in combat.

I was humbled to be in their company. What humbled me the most was their interest in getting me to share my story of time in war. Men who had hundreds of two-way gunfights wanted to know about my time in one. The men I was meeting were America's finest.

I would have opportunities to share my faith in Jesus Christ and how I was coming to believe and why. It was refreshing to speak with special operators who loved Jesus Christ. My time at SOWW birthed a newfound desire to be accountable to a cause greater than myself once more.

The ministry I now have had seeds that were planted over many years cultivating relationships. One such relationship led to a reunion at SOWW. My Ranger buddy Lou Goodman and I had not seen each other since First Battalion's Ranger Ball eighteen years prior. Now we were back together because of SOWW.

Lou and I had served in Third Battalion back when it was the hardest, in the early '90s. When men were Rangers and sheep were scared. When walking with a heavy ruck was our only mode of rapid transportation. This applied to training as well as partying on Victory Drive.

Lou had left B3/75 to return home and work with his family in Wartburg, Tennessee. He had come back into the Army and joined First Battalion in 1999. I was invited to their Ranger Ball in Savannah by Rick Merritt. The guest speaker was Dave Grange. I threw back a few beers with Lou and his men.

Lou would participate in the original incursions made by 1/75 into Afghanistan, before being selected to serve in the greatest Special Mission Unit on the planet. He would spend a long time chasing the men on the list of terrorists we wanted killed or captured.

Lou had distinguished himself as a premier warrior. He is also a premier father, husband, and Ranger buddy. I would not recommend passing out around him if he has an amplifier and electric guitar handy. Nonetheless, Lou and I were now linking up to kill hogs and drink copious amounts of cold beverages.

I would have a successful weekend killing five pigs and winning a few prizes. The friendships will last a lifetime. I met men who have fought in every battle Rangers have fought since Vietnam. I fell in love with cur hunting dogs and the adrenaline involved with chasing wild boar.

I began to heal after a long time separated from the men who gave me everything in life. Being back in a swamp with like-minded men with dogs that kill stuff fed my inner young Ranger. I found the hobby that I would engulf myself in until God calls me home.

Linking up with Lou would end up with long-term implications that have been incredible. I felt God was showing me the next mission. I would dedicate my life to my God. My warrior brothers coming home from war and the SOWW mission of healing warriors, which would become my calling.

I get to talk about Jesus Christ often now. I do not care what men think for I serve the living God, and he speaks to me. He knows all of my shortcomings, and my Ranger brothers accept me for who I am. I am secure in the knowledge that Jesus Christ has saved me for SOWW's purpose.

RLTW
April 10, 2023

# The Obed River

Upon getting home from South Carolina, Susan found us an apartment in downtown Chattanooga on the campus of UTC. We lived on the highest spot above the river. Summer nights were spent listening to concerts simply by opening a window.

We often walked the edge of the river on Chattanooga's walking trail. I enjoyed everything about my time living there, except I had suffered another injury and I was once again taking pills. I had begun hanging out with my buddy who owned a junkyard, just to not be alone.

I was binging on oxycodone and Xanax, and I was so tired of relapse. I had now been an addict longer than I had been straight. I was so ready for a change in permanent venue. I decided I needed to be clean if I was to ever serve God with my whole heart.

I then received a phone call from Lou. He was retiring and moving his family back to Wartburg. He had bought a beautiful piece of property he intended to build his cabin on. Was I interested in coming up and hanging out to check out Morgan County?

We made plans to link up halfway between his house and Chattanooga. He arrived with his son Edward to pick me up and head out to the property. We spent the weekend talking about Ranger life and his missions in Iraq and Afghanistan. My appreciation for his sacrifice grew exponentially.

Meeting his wife turned out to be wonderful as well. Lou and I discussed how I had spent my first years out of the military attending carpentry school and building residential structures. If there was any way I could help, I would get my wife to take a trip up here to visit and decide if MOCO was for us.

Our lease happened to be up in our Chattanooga apartment in one month. I explained to Susan how I felt Morgan County felt conspicuously like Welch, West Virginia. My mother and father-in-law grew up there, and we had visited as family a few times.

The Obed River valley was peaceful and stunning. Lou had introduced me to the owners of the Lilly Pad Hopyard Brewery, and they became my extended family. Susan did not need much persuasion. We wanted a change of scenery, and I needed life to get slower.

We moved our junk into a storage shed in north Georgia near the junkyard. We packed the Escape full to the brim and headed to Deer Lodge, Tennessee, and our rendezvous with the next phase of our lives. Susan and I began exploring the state parks and walking trails immediately.

Susan and I decided we needed to purchase a home. I looked for a few weeks and found none I felt were secluded enough. I needed at least an acre and the end of the road driveway. I wanted the river or a creek to my back. We found a home and made an offer.

We signed the contract and awaited closing. They allowed us to stay in the house to save us some cash before closing. I was beginning to really enjoy the people of Morgan County. Lou and I began hiking the trails on Gobey and on the Obed River by Lilly overlook.

This provided an opportunity to stop in and visit Dale and Martee Scruggs at the Lilly Pad. I spent the next year gracing Dale and Brian Taylor with Wednesday-night darts and beer consumption. We would sip a little shine after the bar had closed and customers were long gone. I woke up there a few times at sunrise.

I was settling in to life in Morgan County. I was spending a lot of time outside. The Obed River was providing an outlet that was not involving narcotics. Lou and I began working on projects at his property. The foundation and walls of the cabin went up as Lou and I were finishing a man cave.

Lou had a few classes to teach, so I used the time exploring the west end of the county. I had been authorized to visit my friend's property in Burrville, Tennessee. Six hundred acres bordered by a state river and state park. I began to want to bowhunt turkey.

I had been offered a chance to attend an event in Alaska where I would join fellow Ranger brothers who served with me in Somalia. We would be staying in Sitka, Alaska, and we would be fishing for salmon and halibut. I decided I had nothing to lose and everything to gain.

I would be rooming with my Ranger buddy Jason Moores. Dave Floyd would be attending, as well as Kevin. This would be epic, being in the company of Rangers alone. Debauchery and games would be on the menu. It was so good seeing Kevin. He became a great Ranger officer who served in harm's way often as a Ranger platoon leader.

This is my first trip abroad with my Ranger brothers since October 3, 1993. Most were fresh home from a deployment to Afghanistan or Iraq at this time in 2016. Spending time with my brothers opened my eyes to just how heroic they have been in keeping us free. I was proud to be in their company once more.

We had an excellent time, and I added a king salmon to my list of fish caught around the world over the course of my life. I returned home with a cooler full of salmon and halibut. I could not wait for spring to get here. I wanted so bad to place a garden for the first time in many years.

I started helping Lou daily. We had a great time getting his home finished for occupation. I was so happy to do my part in helping him find peace after spending so many years prosecuting war. I look forward to many more years at Eagle Ridge man-camp.

Carrie's ghost chicken and dumplings are pretty good as well!

*He was crucified upon a cross of wood, yet he*
*created the hill upon which it stood.*
*He is alive forevermore, and he is returning*
*for his virgin bride very soon.*

RLTW
April 10, 2023

## The Rogue River

After attending the Freedom Alliance–sponsored trip to Sitka, I accepted an invitation to travel to Medford, Oregon, and the mighty Rogue River to fish for steelhead and silver salmon. Two more fish that were on my bucket list for fish caught globally.

I was stepping out in blind faith, trusting that God was indeed ordering my footsteps. I was redeeming the time I had spent alone and away from the community I was a part of for many years now.

God was showing me that my shortcomings just might help another combat veteran not make the same mistakes. I met some very interesting young combat veterans on my first excursion to the Rogue River. We partied, told stories of military service, and caught fish. Mostly, we healed.

I had been to war many years hence. My life had become a minefield for my continuing struggle with addiction. Sharing my struggles and how God brought me through them all began a ministry I did not see coming. The friends I met were telling other veterans my story.

I met an entire new generation of American heroes. I should have known better than to try and hang with their uncanny ability to consume alcohol. By day 3, I had to be left at the lodge to recover from a hangover. I should have never laid down to sleep.

I had begun a conversation with our chaperone. Ryan Beam was himself a veteran. He and I began to share our faith and how we saw the Bible. Seeds were planted in both of our lives. Ryan became indispensable over the next three years. He allowed me to invite Ranger buddies each year after this.

The following year, Ryan reached out to me about the Rogue trip in October. He said Freedom Alliance was wanting Rangers from Mogadishu to fill the trip, and they wanted to bring a cameraman to document our trip. I was really excited about this prospect.

Planning began, and we achieved our goal of filling every slot with a Ranger who survived Mogadishu. Our platoon would have a much-needed rendezvous in Oregon. Some had not seen each other in twenty years. The cameraman was a Marine, and he did an incredible job.

His documentary was played at the Freedom Alliance donor's meeting being attended by executives from Fox News. I was contacted by Ryan Beam about Fox News wanting to do a documentary with the same men who were on the trip to Oregon.

A date was set, and planning began for Eagle Ridge to host Rangers from B3/75 and the film crew from Fox News for the filming of the documentary entitled "Mogadishu: Battalion of Brothers," which eventually debuted on Fox Nation and can be found under the heading "History They Did Not Teach You."

We had an epic week. Our families here in Morgan County got to experience a little bit of our shenanigans learned as young men serving our nation in war and peace. Now we were gathering to share a distinctly American story with a public who most often does not understand the cost of freedom.

It was the first time I was going to share an event that changed me as a human. Whenever I get nervous, I turn to music. I had so many songs on my brain as I began to contemplate God's role in what was happening. I thought about the times on the Megabus visiting friends struggling with trauma from war.

Blaze Foley's song "Clay Pigeons" had taught me empathy in the bus station when I encountered poor people with no money just trying to get home. I was either en route or on my way home from a journey most often to a combat veteran's home to share his grief and guilt and share my testimony.

The song is about the struggles of life and learning empathy. It is an American song written by a songwriter with a heavy heart for others. He seems to be coming to grips with the man he once was and the man he fears becoming. The warrior conundrum.

Blaze decides after encountering a woman with three children that his sorrows are swamped by her reality. It is time to get back in the game and start playing again. Time to once again appreciate each sunrise. It's time to start talking again now that God is telling you what to say.

I now was afforded the opportunity to help my brothers tell a story that America would just soon forget. These men are American heroes, each a part of a very heroic task force and each played a role in the survival of the ones who came home. It was time for fellowship again.

Lou and Carrie Goodman are owed a tremendous debt of gratitude. They hosted us without reservation. I learned a whole lot about why God had saved me for this moment in history. My Ranger brothers proved that we need each other more now than ever.

The Rogue River provided me with the opportunity to say thank you to the men who fought and brought me home. I have found a refuge in the Rogue River valley. I gathered another tool for recovery into my toolbox. I can be myself on the Rogue, and most are unoffended.

There is something to be said about the healing properties of a river and the valley mutually shared. The Rogue River valley tells a tremendous story each time I am found by its majestic banks. Returning each year after the snow melts and the high-water season teaches me about change.

The raging rivers of this life can be a blessing when you allow life to teach the best lessons. Nothing is learned on the mountaintop. It is the valleys of this life that we learn the most about who we really are.

I learned that God has a plan for me to serve the Rangers. This mighty Oregon river provided me an opportunity to share my struggles and my triumphs without reservation. Thank you to those in Oregon who made it all possible. I am eternally indebted for the place and people that helped heal me.

I pray that seeds of salvation in Christ produce a harvest for God's kingdom.

*He was crucified upon a cross of wood, yet he*
*created the hill upon which it stood.*
*He is alive forevermore, and he is returning*
*for his virgin bride very soon.*

RLTW
April 10, 2023

# AS LIVELY STONES

As I contemplated the lessons, I have learned next to the mighty rivers where God has led me, I could not help but include an amazing lesson as timeless as living water itself. While fishing in Oregon last year, God began to show me we are all living stones.

Our time began as an idea from the creator. We were always part of his plan. God illustrates this pattern in the word stones in the Bible. They were always meant to be a source of comfort. Stones sustain all life in the river, continually being washed and ever-changing.

To stand beside a swift moving river and see the energy displayed in the washing of the stones, this occurs where the river is raging hardest, the highest quantity of oxygen anywhere in the river. Where they began their journey is only known by God.

Each stone is different but needed, each having a different journey to this point. Imagine the hardships of each stone, only from the eyes of the other stones. Each stone supports the life of not only every other stone but the living water, and the fish need them to procreate.

To witness a female steelhead migrate to the place where she was born, in the most raging parts of a swollen river, only to begin turning over the stones as she prepares to deposit her eggs, I was beyond fascinated. She laid her eggs where they have the greatest chance of survival.

The stones provide the first comfort for her eggs, waiting to be fertilized by the male making his way upriver. What is it about the fast-moving water and the stones that make it ideal for generation after generation of steelhead?

Even in the most raging water, the stone begins producing sustaining life. As the constant raging waters are polishing it, microscopic algae that are light-sensitive begin to form. These algae grow in amazing circumstances. The raging water strengthens the stem of the algae.

The steelhead returns and flips over the stones with the most algae. They become a heat source and a source of protection from other bacteria, thus providing sustaining life for the embryos. Then comes the male steelhead to fertilize the eggs. The fish hatch, and survival of the fittest begins.

There are no grandparents in the steelhead world. In fact, some male steelhead return to their place of birth to eat the young of other generations. Parenting is the primary focus of the steelhead to ensure their offspring succeed in sustaining life all around them.

There are people who might try to convince you that life is occurring randomly for all. I turn to fish.

Steelhead seem to always make good decisions on survival by living their lives to reproduce and teach the next generation how to live as a provider, protector, and praise leader. The only time that pattern is interrupted in the life of the fish is when humans trick them into swallowing artificial lures.

It is man who gets in the way, not God. God created everything for our benefit. Creation was meant to be the classroom through which God teaches us all, that he holds everything in the palms of his hands. He controls the rivers, the wind, the rain, the sunshine, the storms, agriculture, and our redemption.

If we take the entire human condition, it is not much different than the steelhead world. Some of us are born to a mother and father who only see each other once a year. We end up being raised by grandparents who deserve to be focusing their lives in relationship to the living water.

We begin our lives in the complete chaos of the single-parent household. The river of life begins raging very early in our young existence. Humans have found it easy to mimic the steelhead. Responsibility has left the human conscious. Divorce on demand has destroyed households.

Children are expected to mature with no attachment to the mercy of a father or the grace of a mother. When one is missing, confusion litters every decision in the life of a child. They are being asked to grow up while the river is raging all around them. No one is teaching them about still waters.

In the still waters, the lively stones get a break. It is in still water that sustaining and providing take place constantly. There is a place the rest of the still waters can manifest in each of our lives. It is in the bosom of the Messiah, who is the source of living water.

He is the chief cornerstone of creation. He alone can lead us beside still waters. Only then can we get back to showing unending mercy and unwavering grace with every other stone, regardless of their position in this river. We all are needed to sustain each other.

Whatever label you identify by, God has a place for you in eternity. Labels are men's invention; God believes we are created in his image for the purpose of answering one question in this life. That one question will determine if you make the source of living water your source.

The most preposterous debt payment plan in history was put in motion when our Messiah, king, and high priest crossed the Jordan River, which he had created, to offer himself as a ransom for Israel and a dowry for Gentile hands in marriage.

This story is a love story written on a wooden cross on a lonely hill. The willing Son of God allowed his creation to mock him, scourge him, spit on him, and eventually crucify him. All the while, dumb like a lamb in the mouth of a lion, he opened not his mouth—not even when the nails were driven, the thorns were forced, or the spear went into his side.

Our sin debt to God had been paid by Jesus Christ once for all who would believe!

*He was crucified upon a cross of wood, yet he*
*created the hill upon which it stood.*
*He is alive forevermore, and he is returning*
*for his virgin bride very soon.*

RLTW
April 11, 2023

# THE PEARL OF
# GREAT PRICE

Jesus Christ begins to speak in parables only after his rejection in Matthew 12. The Jews were waiting for the kingdom of David to be established by a militant messiah. The priesthood separated by God to be inclusive had become exclusive. The believing people were very confused.

The purpose of a parable is to bridge a gap of understanding between those who do not get the message and those who are ready to receive the message. They are very simple analogies in speaking and writing that should draw attention to whether we get the message or not.

Jesus begins chapter 13 speaking of a sower who went into a field to sow seed. He continues with different soils that the seed has been sown into. He then talks about wheat and tares: those who get it and those who do not. He explains to all that if you believe, you must become a sower of seed.

The soil is the human condition, all kinds depending on how good or bad life without God has been. God is the one who prepares soil to receive the seed of the word of God. We are to become sowers of the seed. The seeds are mercy and grace. Love is summed up in these godly attributes.

God's love requires that we focus on the one providing the love. To the Christian, love must become about focusing on others by becoming stewards of the written word of God. Our world is seeking a messiah, and it is our calling to offer them ours, even to the point of persecution.

The sixth parable is directed at what drives men mad. The Bible states you cannot serve God and money. So often we are taught by

Jesus Christ what is the product of belief in him, and persecution is the exact opposite of prosperity. This parable deals directly with those who get paid to preach.

Jesus Christ introduces us to the pearl of great price. The Hebrew mind would have scoffed, for the pearl is produced by an unclean species of shellfish. He was speaking to the religious leaders holding the people hostage to dietary restrictions and religious legalism.

These men were now selling the offerings the Hebrews were to bring willingly to the temple, regardless of their position in society. God had given them a way for all people to achieve forgiveness, and they now were selling the offerings.

They had become money changers and were married to the capitalist system they had been called out of. Only Judas got paid for the message of Christ's Crucifixion. It did not work out well for him.

Jesus Christ is teaching how the kingdom of God begins, who is really in, and what they are willing to live without to possess the knowledge of him. He is asking them if they are willing to experience riches in this life, in exchange for torment in the next.

The message of Jesus Christ always has been about redeeming time in our lives and the life of the creation currently in bondage because of Lucifer's rebellion and our soon-after falling from grace. God's war has always been with the fallen angel in charge of chaos in our world.

We are pawns in a cosmic love drama written by God, to prove he alone is sovereign over creation. His battle is against Lucifer and his fallen-angel army. We were created to reproduce and replace the fallen angels with believers whom we had shown the way of mercy and grace.

The story of the merchant who finds a pearl of great price and sells everything he has to retain the pearl is our testimony.

How many people understand that a pearl begins as an irritation within an unclean species? That irritation becomes completely desirable by some willing to undergo transformation. The ministry of Christ began with his family as a young boy with irritation.

He was despised by his own family until after his resurrection, where we find at least two of his siblings martyred by the Herods in

Jerusalem. It would seem they had made Jesus Christ their pearl of great price. They gave all to include their lives to advance his message.

We are all merchants of some sort in this life. We sow corruption or blessing, no middle ground. We all have something we are keeping from our creator. He knows our thoughts before we think them. His desire is to bring peace into our world, and the world sows division.

When I made the decision that I would abandon everything this life has to offer and trust only in the truths of the Bible, life really began to make sense, and I could learn to love God and others again.

Addiction has manifested now in my love of hunting dogs. I have seven varieties of cur. They love going after anything with four legs. They are how I have found peace in God's provision. I have something smarter than me to learn from once again, just like the Rangers I took to war.

My wife asked me, "Why seven?" I said seven represents the heptadic structure the entire Bible is written in no matter which language you choose. It is God's fingerprint on his owner's manual and life-warranty deed.

She asked, "Why the affinity for dogs and not humans?"

My response was simple: Dogs cannot pretend to love you!

I had to learn over time to trust and love humans again. I am a work in progress. For now, I have Daisy, Dixie, Betsy Ross, Maximus, Ahab, Jezebel, and Waingro to trounce through the mountains and rivers with as God redeems the time the locust had eaten in my life.

I am forever a glass-half-full guy. The rivers taught me how to survive, whether raging all around or in the calm of the storm. I know my redeemer lives!

*He was crucified upon a cross of wood, yet he*
*created the hill upon which it stood.*
*He is alive forevermore, and he is returning*
*for his virgin bride very soon.*

RLTW
April 11, 2023

# THE LIVING WATER

Sticking with a theme of literature and ancient languages, what does ancient Hebrew teach us about living water? Moses was given revelation of Torah in the ancient Hebrew language. God the creator spoke Hebrew. This is the ancient language of my mother's ancestors.

Hebrew is made up of twenty-two characters. It is labeled a semimic language. It is a language produced by guttural inflection. It is the language designed by God to sing his praises as creator. Hebrew is the language designed to praise God.

Each character tells an individual story of its own. Beginning with the *aleph* and ending with the *tau*, each Hebrew letter has a corresponding numerical value. The Old Testament sems to have been conceived by God in language and mathematical application to understanding the creation.

The first letter aleph is the first letter in the creation name of God. The aleph is the symbol of the ox. The ox is both a burden bearer and animal sacrificed religiously by men. God the creator begins his name by stating "I am the burden bearer to be sacrificed religiously by men."

The aleph happens to also represent the first created deity worshipped continuously by men and women. In paganism, the ox is represented by the bull. The bull is worshipped by societies as being the source of monetary provision and military might.

Every ancient civilization has mythologies where bulls are worshipped and sacrificed before military engagements. America is no different. The cult of Mithras is alive and well on Wall Street. This is the Roman rendering of the cults who worship the bronze bull.

The tau is the twenty-second letter in the Hebrew alphabet. It is a cross-shaped mark. In English, it is our letter *T*. The tau is the place Christ our creator died to pay the sin debt of all humanity. The tau litters the Old Testament for the cross was always the plan of our creator.

The tau was the mark placed upon the being of Cain, prior to God sending him into the world, without the ability to be killed. Was Cain the first biblical evangelist? He did carry the cross with him wherever he went. He did have God's covering over his life. God alone controlled when Cain died.

What does the creation name of God reveal in the Hebrew tongue about the source of true living water? In Hebrew, the creation name of God transliterates as *Elohim*—aleph, lahmed, heh, yod, mem. I will focus on the *mem*.

In Hebrew transliterations to English, whenever there is an *M* at the end of a word, we are dealing with a duality. This is a plural pronoun expressed in singular terms. In Hebrew, Egypt is labeled *Mizraim*, the land of the two rivers: one Egypt, Upper and Lower Nile.

In Hebrew, a duality is most often three in one. The creation name of God is no different. We have covered the aleph as the ox or burden bearer to be sacrificed, which is the first letter in the name of God the Father. El is the burden bearer to be sacrificed who carries the shepherd's staff.

The lahmed or *L* in English is a shepherd's staff. It has only two ends and describes the divine attributes of God the creator, one end representing eternal mercy, the other end for unwavering grace. One deals with a willingness to undergo biblical correction, the other deals with biblical restoration.

God uses shepherds consistently throughout biblical history to illustrate his desire to become our divine shepherd.

His offer of mercy and grace is alive today because of the cross and the empty tomb. The only requirement for eternal life is to acknowledge we are not God and that we have gone astray like sheep and we need our shepherd to provide his life as our dowry.

Recognize that the Trinity of creation became a man, and all for the purpose of dying so he could be with us for all eternity. Love has nothing to do with judgment. Love is bound by eternal mercy and unwavering grace. Love was provided by the living water who still provides refreshing!

The last letter in the creation name of God is the mem. It is the symbol of living water. It begins the Hebrew title of Jesus, the Mashiach Nagid—the Messiah and king of the earth. His name begins as the source of true living water, both in the natural and spiritual.

The living water proceeded forth from the Messiah's side as he gave up the Ghost. Do you realize the Ghost had to leave Jesus for us to receive the second person of the Trinity, the Holy Spirit? The source of living water is Messiah crucified, and the messenger is the Ruach HaKodesh or Holy Spirit.

The heh is the Spirit of God. It is the third letter in his creation name. It is represented by an open window to God the creator. It is given to all those who have the audacity to not care what men think and only focus on what Elohim did for all of us.

The miracle of the Bible is that the language it is understood matters not. The miracle of Hebrew, a symbol language being transliterated into the conquest language of English and still be understood by common humans, baffles me.

The Bible is sixty-six books, revealed to at least forty scribes over 3,000 years, all pointing to ELOHIM our creator suspended between heaven and earth, only to walk out of a rich man's borrowed tomb to declare that he alone is creation's source of living water.

It has been the journey of a lifetime realizing that God's desire is to seek us. He is chasing us! All the while, we submit to the religious traditions of men, which cannot save one soul. We are offered the chance to be born again in God's image.

That image is who he is, not what he does. It is summed up in the love language of Hebrew.

"I am the aleph and the tau. I am the alpha and omega. I am the first and the last. I am living water!"

*He was crucified upon a cross of wood, yet he*
*created the hill upon which it stood.*
*He is alive forevermore, and he is returning*
*for his virgin bride very soon.*

RLTW
April 11, 2023

# SPECIAL OPERATIONS WOUNDED WARRIORS

The year 2016 was my official homecoming. The community I once served was asking me to serve once more, but not before welcoming me home.

It had been twenty-three years since I returned from Mogadishu, Somalia, injured. It had been a long time since I had toasted the men I lost and brothers I never got to say goodbye to. This organization exists to find men like me, brothers-in-arms who somehow got lost on the road after doing exactly what their creed requires. Somewhere along the way, I had stopped Rangering. Or so I thought.

I was a United States Army Airborne Ranger. I spent five years in a rifle company in the Seventy-Fifth Ranger Regiment. I would dare to say it's the best Ranger rifle company the regiment has ever seen. I was one bearing in the gears of Bravo Company that when in time, made the whole engine work. Bravo Company was home to me, and the men I served with are my family. The DNA that makes up our family can never be manipulated. It is a blood covenant.

Rangers serve at the behest of the president. They are as close to tier 1 as any unit gets. While not always enjoying the budgets of other Special Operations units, no unit has been asked to do more for our country. And Bravo Company has led the way every time.

On Rio Hata in Panama, Bravo Company 3/75 lost Staff Sergeant Larry Bernard and Private First Class Roy Brown, with Bill Dunham and Patrick Kilgallen suffering injuries that still remind them each day of their sacrifice. These men are the reason I served.

I had the privilege of welcoming these men home from the hospital in 1990. I have remained a steadfast advocate for my brothers, and my best friend in life served in their platoon in Panama. Paul Mercer is the greatest Ranger and best American I have ever met and called my friend.

I remained in B3/75 for five years. I served in positions ranging from Mortar Section FDC chief, team leader in a rifle platoon, squad leader of a rifle squad, and culminating in my job in Somalia as Weapons Squad leader, Third Platoon B3/75 Ranger Regiment. The greatest privilege the Lord Jesus Christ ever bestowed upon me was the privilege to lead Rangers in combat. Nothing since has kept my attention.

In Somalia, I had an amazing group of men in my squad. My three machine gunners were all better than me at being a daily Ranger. Dominic Pilla, Chris Schlief, and Dave Ritchie are three amazing Americans. Dominic would die in Somalia leading with led and killing his killer. Chris Schlief was unwavering in Mogadishu and the most brilliant man I have ever encountered. He has continued to serve our country in Special Operations, and today he is a command sergeant major in a Special Forces group. Dave Ritchie was my gunner on my vehicle on October 3, 1993. He is my hero. He was wounded early in the mission and continued to fight with an M16 after his machine gun was disabled. Dave ended up leading our vehicle home when I was wounded near the front of the convoy for the third time. Dave was a spec4 in Somalia.

I had my gunner Clay Othic wounded seriously with the loss of his shooting arm. Lorenzo Ruiz took over the .50 caliber and was fatally wounded taking over from Clay Othic. I was wounded once by gunfire early and once by shrapnel before I was hit the third time making my way back through the convoy toward my vehicle. That left a spec4 in charge of my vehicle team and the rear of the convoy. Dave Ritchie was able to lead them for two hours as we fought our way back to our base. Dave Ritchie would go on to serve in Task Force 160th as a CH-47 pilot for every year of the Global War on Terror. He retired as chief warrant officer 4 and continues to serve his state as a pilot fighting forest fires in California. He is an American Special Operations hero.

Chad Fowles was an assistant machine gunner for Dave Ritchie and drove our vehicle. He somehow managed to not get hit in Somalia. God has a plan for Chad Fowles, and I pray SOWW helps him find it. Chad retired as a master sergeant with twenty years in the Army. Along for the ride on my vehicle was Private First Class Jason Dancy. He also managed to not get hit, but it does not diminish his contribution to the regiment and Bravo Company lure. He fought like a Spartan on October 3, 1993. Reese Teakell was Chris Schlief's new ammo bearer in Somalia. His first deployment in Bravo Company was to Somalia. Reese went on to serve the regiment after returning from Somalia in every position from team leader to squad leader to command sergeant major of the Special Troops Battalion. He is today a command sergeant major in a brigade of the Eighty-Second Airborne Division. Ed Kallman rounds out Weapons Squad who fought on October 3, 1993. He was the driver for another vehicle and managed to not get wounded. I was privileged to lead these men in support of the Special Operations mission to Somalia. I intend to work tirelessly to bring these men home to SOWW and back together as a Ranger family.

I left the Army in 1995. I was a platoon sergeant in Vicenza, Italy, a final act of mercy from a loving God. I got to share with my platoon in Italy the lives of my squad and their heroism in service to the regiment and SOCCOM. I live every day for the chance to share my life and its struggles with my Ranger brothers, and SOWW is the platform that continues to make it possible.

As the country debates our nation's path forward, there's one thing that is undebatable: The true 1 percent of Americans that should be recognized are the 1 percent of Americans that have actually volunteered to defend the American life we enjoy on battlefields most Americans know not exist. When you break it down further, less than 1/10 of 1 percent of those ever serve in a Special Mission Unit. The freedom we all profess comes at a cost that continues to be paid for by the 1/10 of 1 percent of Americans who get to call themselves the SOCCOM family. It is a family that can never be divided, and SOWW is the greatest mechanism for keeping the family recognized and together as we embark on the next phase of our lives.

America has once again become apathetic to all things military. We can never surrender. If we surrender, this entire experiment of a government of the people, for the people, and by the people will perish from the earth.

SOWW exists to make sure America never forgets the lives led by Rangers, SEALs, operators, and airmen who continue to provide America with a blanket of protection. The freedom we enjoy is because of men who serve in SOCCOM. SOWW is the place where SOCCOM family reunions continue to occur.

I was privileged to meet a man I now can identify as my brother while attending a SOWW event in South Carolina. I was stepping out in extreme faith by attending this event. My Ranger brother, and survivor of Mogadishu, Dave Floyd had invited me to the annual SOWW hogg hunt called Takin' Bacon. I accepted, and boy was God a gracious God. Not only did I connect with men I had served with, I got to meet an entire generation of special men who had now served our country in a protracted war with no end in sight. But one I will never forget: Eddie Oglesby was one of the dog handlers. I felt there was something more to Eddie, so I struck up a conversation with him. Eddie had served our nation in Vietnam as a Ranger in Papa Company Seventy-Fifth Infantry. He and I were DNA brothers, and we were meeting at SOWW. I sensed Eddie was experiencing his own sort of homecoming. SOWW was the mechanism by which Eddie and I connected, and we will be brothers who look forward to Takin' Bacon every year. I miss Eddie every day. He taught me more about responsibility to my brothers than any shrink could ever hope to learn in twenty years of practice. SOWW did that for me and an old Ranger from Vietnam who came home to a divided nation. Imagine the Rangers coming home now.

SOWW provides special men with the opportunity to share their experiences with people who will be able to show empathy rather than sympathy. The stories would never be understood by a public that has lost its sense of understanding of freedom's high cost. Special Operations Wounded Warriors caters to the needs of men who have been wounded defending our ideals as Judeo-Christian

Americans. Our creeds are our bond and promise to this nation. Our experiences in war are our bond to each other.

SOWW has put its money where its mouth is. Warriors from the SOCCOM community gather each year in March to fellowship, kill wild boar, and party like it's 1999. The place where this occurs costs money every year to lease. We at SOWW have been afforded the opportunity to purchase the property and make it a permanent destination throughout the year for men and families in our very small community who have borne the brunt of this protracted war on terror. It will never end, and our mission to our community will never end. Consider giving a monetary gift to further our mission from once a year to permanent status. The property along the river comes at a cost of three million dollars.

I know the Ranger community alone could raise that! This organization is limiting the damage to warriors in our community who need us to continue the family bonds into eternity. We have borne the brunt of the freedom debt our country expects us to continue to pay. Please help us reach our goal.

Donations to our cause should be sent via www.sowwcharity. com. Please prayerfully consider helping our cause. It is our nation's cause!

*He was crucified upon a cross of wood, yet he*
*created the hill upon which it stood.*

RLTW
June 9, 2020

\*\*\*\*\*

*A portion of the proceeds from the sale of every book will be donated to Special Operations Wounded Warriors in the name of Daniel D. Busch.*

*A portion of the proceeds will also go to Behind the Veil Ministries in the name of CW2 Aaron A. Weaver—my Ranger brother, an American hero, and a friend to all things Jesus Christ.*

*The rest of the proceeds will support Gold Star programs supported by the USSOCCOM community. We owe these family members continued support as they navigate this life without the brothers we served with. Rangers lead the way!*

# BRIDGES

As I finished writing *The Rivers of My Life*, I was exhausted. I had successfully redeemed the time I had lost in unbelief. All those years I spent running from God, and I had to find out the hardest ways that He is a God who delights in making and keeping His promises.

He had called me at the age of ten. The shining one had a road map by which he intended to destroy me. It was not because of me, but because God wanted to use me. The sovereignty of God has been on full display no matter how hard I tried to separate from his love.

As I contemplated the ending to telling my story, littered with land mines and human challenges, it occurred to me that God has a sovereign plan for those who profess faith in Jesus Christ. It has to do with inclusion, not exclusion. Denominational Christianity screams "I am exclusive."

*The Rivers of My Life* had exposed completely the human condition from the creator's perspective. We are all sinners. We all need God's debt payment plan for our lives. We all need waters of refreshing. The living water is the Messiah who purchased our redemption, the most misunderstood rabbi in history.

My conclusions have led me to form a new approach to my ministry aspirations. I had to ask, Is the message of Jesus Christ inclusive or exclusive? This is a loaded question.

From the perspective of how preposterous the plan is, Jesus Christ's message is exclusive.

From the perspective of what was accomplished on Calvary, Christ's offer of unending mercy leading to unwavering grace in our lives is the most inclusive message in human history.

Religion has hijacked what God promised and planned from before the beginning of recorded history. The Crucifixion was a preplanned mission from the Trinity who spoke our universe into existence. It happens to be the greatest conspiracy theory I have ever believed.

Understand that the creator of our entire universe entered our created world in the womb of a virgin Jewish girl, not to live but fully knowing the exact hour he would give up the Ghost and pay the only debt that matters when I die. He died so I might live!

I decided I would follow his example on the cross when Jesus Christ was suspended between heaven and earth. Judgment was the furthest thing from his mind as he offered one thief mercy and the other grace! These alone are God's desire for humanity.

I decided something needed to change, and that something was how I saw what Christ did for me. Until I grasped that God the Creator was on that cross and He was on there for me, there would be no ability to understand what God wanted me to do with the knowledge of my own personal salvation.

I have worn many hats in this life. My black beret earned as a Ranger is my favorite. God had another hat I earned in the construction field, a hard hat. I was to take my knowledge of construction and apply it to my ministry. I was to become a teacher, but first I had to learn to love God's students.

It would be easy to accept that all I have endured was simply due to bad judgment. Anyone who knows me would say that is half the equation. The other half had to do with God ordering my footsteps which brought me to this point. My mistakes are what God gave me to help others in this hour.

Every river, every hard decision, every broken heart, and every lost brother were all part of God's permissive will for my life. It is my story; it is my song. Now what do I do with it?

I only know three things: lead, follow, or get the f—— out of the way! It is the Ranger way. I've never been good at following, and I've never gotten out of the way of anything. I had only one left: LEAD!

My life has always been a story of a bridge builder in the making. I have always been the guy who loves the underdog. Today, when

I choose a puppy to raise, I always take the runt. No one ever wants the runt, yet I have found the secret is in the least becoming the best!

This is the story of God our creator. He takes the least of us and makes us the most. To become the most, you must first become the least. To become the new creation, old things pass away, and all things become new. This applied to human religion in my life.

I have no time to worry about what men think in this life, for I spend all my time learning what God thinks in scripture. I know now God thinks he completely loves his creation, and his desire is for us to teach others just how much God loves them.

You cannot show mercy while judging others! Mercy and judgment are opposites. They cannot coexist. Christ's message of mercy is inclusive. Judgment leads to exclusion and can turn more people away from this great plan than it will ever produce souls saved!

God's perfect, pleasing will is for all men to come to the knowledge of Jesus Christ. To come to this knowledge, the Berean path taught by Paul in Acts 17:11 is the only way a Christian can avoid religious deception and become a bridge builder for Christ's kingdom.

Bridge building in God's kingdom is all about the message of mercy still being offered by the risen bridegroom over creation. Today I must show mercy to everyone I encounter. When I was in sin, I knew it. I never needed to be told that what I was doing separated me from my relationship to God.

What I needed was Christian mercy! I needed just one church person to tell me Christ loved me despite myself. I needed them to be Christian, not just talk about it. This has become my life's calling. I teach the entire Bible, and I leave church to those who have decided on a path of exclusion.

Today I build bridges to help people cross rivers that may seem too wild or too swollen to cross by themselves. The key is having the humility to always pray for the unending mercy of God over my life so that grace may appear in the lives of others.

Bridge building is about serving a cause greater than myself. I now build only bridges of perfect love as shown us by Christ on that lonely hill, where the willing Son of God died to pay the only debt that matters in my life when I die. My sin debt to God as my creator!

*He was crucified upon a cross of wood, yet he
created the hill upon which it stood.
He is alive forevermore, and he is returning
for his virgin bride very soon.*

In Christ's service,
May 30, 2023

# EPILOGUE

As I contemplated coming to the end of my river journey, emotions I had not held for a long time gripped me. Redeeming time is about confronting where you've been, where you are at, and where you are going. We are in the world, but not of the world.

My life is no different than most in post–World War II America. Prosperity and pride led to apostasy and unbridled lawlessness away from biblical morality. Our two-party system set about engineering a world where demigods decide who prospers and which religions are tolerated.

My life is one where I challenged every social norm from birth until today. I am an insurrectionist. Quickest way to get me motivated is to remind me what I cannot do. Most great decisions begin for me the same way every time: Hold my beer and watch this shit! I do not recommend this approach.

David met Goliath in the valley of Elah. This is the valley of the oak trees. The analogy and setting point to the hardness of the oak tree in reference to decisions made by Israel and Saul that differ from decisions made by David. This illustration is about hard choices.

There's a glaring difference between two men, both anointed by the prophet God sent—different destinies with interwoven paths, with one who leaned on his own understanding and failed God in cleansing the land of the fallen-angel offspring. Goliath is the first of five giants Daniel planned to deal with.

God had delivered many enemies into Saul's hands. Saul began to see his victories through prideful eyes as he failed to follow God's command to kill Agag, king of Israel's most consistent enemy. The Amalekites gave us Haman the Agagite in the court of Queen Esther in Persia.

The Amalekites were the first enemy to come out against Moses and Aaron in the Negev desert of southern Israel. Amalekites formed the National Socialist Party in Germany and birthed Hitler. Ten Amalekites were executed on Purim in 1946 as prophesied by Esther.

I fear Amalekites escaped Nazi Germany with the help of the Popes and bishops of the Roman Catholic church who have set up shop in every nation where Catholicism exists. America smuggled 3,500 Nazi war criminals to America for their knowledge and educational experiences. PhDs placed Jews in ovens!

All these truths were part of confronting the narrative that surrounded everything I was shown or taught growing up. I was raised Roman Catholic in a home with a father and stepmother. There was always something missing that my stepmother tried to fill as a void.

I rebelled most often because I read the Bible as my first rebellion against family and priests at school. I could not understand why they did not allow access to the Bible. I began to read my father's *Latin Vulgate* very young, and all I was seeing were people justifying bad behavior with nonbiblical beliefs.

I was reading about a Jewish rabbi named Jesus Christ in the Western-believing world. I was understanding things that scared me. God was just, and the Bible was pointing out that his justice does have a time limit.

In my own life, God had always been there. I was too busy trying to ascend the mountains faster than anyone to realize he desired I exist in the valley, where I am most often forced to acknowledge him in failure. It is in the valleys of life that God meets those he loves.

It is in these valleys that rivers of refreshing become real. I set out to discover Jesus Christ's role in creation, and the rivers have taught me so much about this equation we label life. I realized that my life proved he is indeed the most misunderstood rabbi in history.

His kingship, promised to Mary in her womb, has been relegated to nominally spiritual. The written revealed word of God has been replaced by religious traditions and doctrines of men. Outward piety replaced the continuous offering of mercy and grace the Crucifixion promised.

Corporate religion has replaced faith in homes where the original church was started. I fear we have lost our first love. I fear Jesus Christ weeps each time a believer questions their faith after receiving his promises. I realized early on that my relationship to God meant I had to leave the land of my nativity.

This story is indeed about God always being there. He knows my end from my beginning. My faith in him is about understanding the mercy I require each day as one of history's greatest sinners. I am the product of unending mercy and unwavering grace. This is my faith.

It is in a God-man who was born to learn what I was going through. His destiny was to die for the sins of humanity. His inheritance is to sit upon David's throne in Jerusalem, judging all the nations of the earth in righteousness. Peace like a river will flow from the mercy seat of our risen Messiah.

God's throne will once again be among men in Israel. Jesus Christ will indeed return with his bride to usher in the millennial kingdom of our God and Savior, Yeshua Hamashiach.

Crossing the Jordan River after being removed to heaven at the rapture is my future hope in Jesus Christ. I am preparing to meet my risen bridegroom by offering all the mercy and grace he first offered me. I have removed the foreign gods from my life, and the Trinity is who I worship alone.

Christianity was never supposed to be the majority opinion. To love those who despitefully use you is not for everyone, yet it alone is the measure of salvation. How much you love Jesus Christ comes through in how much you can love the unlovable!

It has been the honor of my life to traverse these mighty rivers while going though incredible valleys in this life. The mountaintop is no longer my goal. I cry out to God in the valley, and I never want to forget that again! I will leave the mountaintops for the next generation.

I pray this story helps just one person understand that there is a God who loves his creation!

## JOHN BURNS

*He was crucified upon a cross of wood, yet he*
*created the hill upon which it stood.*
*He is alive forevermore, and he is returning*
*for his virgin bride very soon.*

I love you all in Christ,
RLTW

# ABOUT THE AUTHOR

John Burns is a staff writer at the *Morgan County Today* newspaper, the chaplain of Special Operations Wounded Warriors nonprofit, and the president of Behind the Veil Ministries Inc.

His Christian faith is the foundation for every aspect of his life. He is married to Susan C. Burns of Lancing, Tennessee. He is blessed with four grown children: Sean, Andrew, Kasey, and Lisa. He also has eleven wonderful grandchildren.

His hobbies include turkey hunting, hound dogs, hogg hunting, beer tasting, coffee drinking, and studying the Bible every day.

His ministry to the Special Operations community was born out of his desire to serve the community that gave him so much in life.

"The men who came before me were giants. They led the way and ensured we would give it one hell of a go. I have so many to thank. The only way I know how is to serve them tirelessly so we can all fellowship forever on the other side of glory."

The road goes on forever, and the party never ends...

He was crucified upon a cross of wood, yet he created the hill upon which it stood.

www.ingramcontent.com/pod-product-compliance
Lightning Source LLC
LaVergne TN
LVHW020752170125
801451LV00021B/446